Rough Carpentry and Masonry

Rough Carpentry and Masonry

Henry F. Atkinson

Former Occupations Instructor
Glendale High School
Tillsonburg, Ontario

McGraw-Hill Ryerson Limited

Toronto Montreal New York St. Louis San Francisco
Auckland Bogotá Guatemala Hamburg Johannesburg
Lisbon London Madrid Mexico New Delhi Panama
Paris San Juan São Paulo Singapore Sydney Tokyo

ROUGH CARPENTRY AND MASONRY,
Second Edition SI Metric

Copyright © McGraw-Hill Ryerson Limited, 1981
Copyright © McGraw-Hill Company of Canada Limited, 1969
ISBN 0-07-548013-1

1 2 3 4 5 6 7 8 9 0 D 0 9 8 7 6 5 4 3 2 1

Printed and bound in Canada

CANADIAN CATALOGUING IN PUBLICATION DATA

Atkinson, Henry F., date
  Rough carpentry and masonry

Includes index.
ISBN 0-07-548013-1

1. House construction. 2. Carpentry. 3. Masonry.
I. Title.

TH4815.A8 1981   690   C81-094300-X

Contents

INTRODUCTION

While this book is being published, Canada is in the process of changing its entire system of measurement. The Canadian Standards Association, the Canadian Standards Council, and a special Metric Commission are establishing new standards in cooperation with industry.

The world needs a common system of measurement. The need for this new system is the direct result of our modern worldwide transportation and communications network. The markets for our industrial, agricultural and lumber production are found in all parts of the world. When we sell to other countries, they require sizes and quantities that are familiar to them. The same is true for us when we import goods.

Our old inch-pound system of measurement was not a good one for all nations to adopt. There were too many oddly-related units in it. In distance measurement alone, there were miles, chains, rods, yards, feet and inches. These could in turn be divided into fractions, each with a name of its own.

Many other countries had developed systems of measurement based completely on multiples of ten, known as "metric" systems. Although all of these systems made use of the same idea, some of the units of measurement were different from country to country. A meeting was held in 1960 with representatives from many nations to decide on a single standard metric system. The system decided upon is called the *International System of Units* and is abbreviated **SI**. It is hoped that all countries will, in time, adopt the SI system.

SI METRIC FOR THE BUILDING TRADES

SI Metric is a decimal system. Its units can be multiplied or divided by ten to form larger or smaller measures. This means that measuring can be done simply by moving the decimal point to the right when multiplying and to the left when dividing. For example, ten millimetres equal one centimetre, and thirty-six millimetres equal three and six-tenths centimetres (36 mm = 3.6 mm). A unit can be multiplied or divided by any multiple of ten. These multiples and divisions have names and symbols that indicate their values:

Name	Symbol	Value
micro	μ	1/1 000 000
milli	m	1/1000
centi	c	1/100
deci	d	1/10
deca	da	10
hecto	h	100
kilo	k	1000
mega	M	1 000 000

These names or symbols are used as prefixes. They are placed before a unit name or symbol and attached to it. For example, a centimetre is one one-hundredth of a metre, and 2 km = 2000 m. Note that in writing out the number you must also write out the prefix and unit, but if a number symbol is used, you must use the prefix and unit symbols.

DISTANCE MEASUREMENT

The *metre* (m) is the standard unit of distance. The dimensions on building drawings are standard in either metres or *millimetres* (mm) but both do not appear on the same drawing. Lumber thickness and width are given in millimetres while length is stated in metres. The area of surfaces such as floors and roofs is calculated in square metres (m^2).

MEASUREMENT OF MASS

The SI unit of mass is the *kilogram* (kg). Notice that this unit already includes the prefix. *Mass* is not another word for *weight*. The mass of an object is the amount of matter that makes up that object. An object with a certain mass on earth will be the same object with the same mass if taken to the moon. Weight however, is the measure of the downward force of an object caused by the pull of gravity on it. Since the moon's gravity is less than the earth's, an object will weigh less on the moon. A stack of bricks on a skid has both *mass* and *weight* (the force of the bricks pushing down on the skid). These two terms should be used carefully to describe what you want to say accurately.

MEASUREMENT OF VOLUME AND CAPACITY

Volume describes the space that something takes up, while the word *capacity* describes how much of something a container can hold. Both volume and capacity may be measured in cubic metres (m^3), cubic centimetres (cm^3), or litres (L). Note that one cubic centimetre is equal to one millilitre (1 cm^3 = 1 mL).

MEASUREMENT OF TEMPERATURE

The Celsius temperature scale is standard in SI Metric. Its symbol is °C. No prefixes are used with this symbol. On the Celsius scale, 0°C indicates the freezing point of water, and 100° the boiling point.

METRIC MEASUREMENT IN THE NEAR FUTURE

The old inch-pound system will not suddenly disappear. It will take time to wear out our old tools and machinery, and for industry to equip factories to produce machinery and materials to the new standards. The cost of replacing equipment on such a large scale is too great for it to happen all at once. At any rate, although many of the new SI standards for building construction have been decided upon, there are still decisions to be made. Building materials are now being produced to the new standards, but you can expect to see lumber, plywood and other materials still designed to the inch-pound system for several years to come.

The dimensions and other references to measurement in this text-book conform to SI Metric standards so that students can begin to learn and use the system while they learn about construction methods. However, for three topic areas—cubic measure of concrete, calculating board measure, and roof framing—sections on Imperial measurement, with illustrations, have been added. Since calculations with the Imperial system may still be necessary in the near future, it is hoped that these sections will provide useful information.

In addition, comparative reference charts for lumber and nail sizes appear below. Students will still need to recognize Imperial measurements when purchasing these materials.

The following list provides the references sources used in the preparation of this book.

From the Canadian Standards Association:
Building Drawings Can 3-878.3-M77
Burned Clay Brick A82.1-M1977 (SI Units)
Asphalt Coated Roofing Sheets A123.2-M1979
Asphalt or Tar Saturated Roofing Felt A123.3-M1979
CSA Standards on Concrete Masonry Units A165-M1977

From the Canadian Wood Council:
Metric Manual for Wood Products
Metric Span Tables for Wood Joists, Rafters and Beams

From the Canadian Lumbermen's Association:
Metric Handbook for Canadian Softwood Lumber

From the Clay Brick Association of Canada:
Technical Notes on Brick Construction based on CSA Can 3-Z234.1-
1976 and Can 3-A31.M-1975

From the National Concrete Producers' Association:
Introducing Metric Concrete Masonry Units

From the Canadian Portland Cement Association:
Design and Control of Concrete Mixtures, Metric Edition

The author also wishes to acknowledge the kind assistance given
by the Construction Materials Group of Domtar Inc. and Building Products of Canada Limited.

Table 1. Metric and Imperial Lumber Sizes

Metric Dimensions (mm)	Nominal Imperial Size (in.)	Metric Dimensions (mm)	Nominal Imperial Size (in.)
19 × 38	1 × 2	38 × 38	2 × 2
19 × 64	1 × 3	38 × 64	2 × 3
19 × 89	1 × 4	38 × 89	2 × 4
19 × 114	1 × 5	38 × 114	2 × 5
19 × 140	1 × 6	38 × 140	2 × 6
19 × 165	1 × 7	38 × 165	2 × 7
19 × 184	1 × 8	38 × 184	2 × 8
19 × 235	1 × 10	38 × 235	2 × 10
19 × 286	1 × 12	38 × 286	2 × 12
19 × 337	1 × 14	38 × 337	2 × 14
19 × 387	1 × 16	38 × 387	2 × 16

Table 2. Metric and Imperial Nail Sizes

Metric Length* (mm)	Imperial Length (in.)
25	1
38	1½
45	1¾
50	2
65	2½
75	3
90	3½
100	4
150	6
300	12

*Note: It is expected that when industry standardizes its metric nail sizes, those sizes will be "hard converted" to the nearest millimetre, and where possible, to the nearest 5 mm or 10 mm. For example, the 1¾ in. nail will be 45 mm, not 44.5 mm or 44 mm. This style has been used in this textbook.

CHAPTER **1**

House Building Styles

WATCH FOR THESE WORDS

blueprint
subdivision
dormer
by-laws

HOW TO USE THESE WORDS

1. The **blueprints** of a house show all of the drawings needed to build it.
2. New houses in a **subdivision** must be built to certain standards.
3. A **dormer** is a window used to let daylight into an attic room.
4. The **by-laws** of a town control all construction within the town limits.

FIND THE ANSWERS TO THESE QUESTIONS

1. Why are houses that are built from the same blueprints often very different in appearance?
2. Study the drawings and photos of single-storey houses and list the features that make each one different from the others.

3. List two reasons why two-storey houses provide more living space for the money than other house styles.

4. What do you think are the reasons for the popularity of split-level houses?

When you mention building construction, most people immediately picture in their minds the perfect house for themselves. Since each person has definite likes and dislikes as well as financial limits, the style and size of another person's dream house will probably be quite different from yours. This individuality gives each house its own special appearance even though it might have been built from the same **blueprint** as another one down the street.

As you will see in this chapter, there are very few basic styles of houses, yet our streets and **subdivisions** rarely appear monotonous unless the builder has failed to use his imagination. With so much variety in building materials today, it is possible to give every house its own style. Study the drawings and photographs in this chapter.

ONE-STOREY HOUSES

Small one-storey houses are often called cottages, while the large sprawling models are known as ranch-style homes. Many people prefer ranch-style homes because there are no stairs to climb, but the larger houses need large building lots which are expensive and often not available. The one-storey house generally costs more to build than any of the other styles if you compare the amount of living space.

blueprint: A photographic print with white lines on a blue background. Also used to mean a blue line print with a white background.

subdivision: A large area of land divided into building lots.

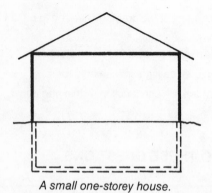

A small one-storey house.

A one-storey ranch-style house.

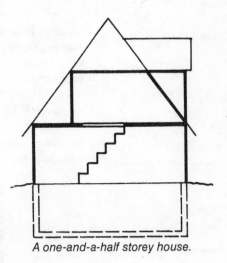

A one-storey house with a flat roof.

ONE-AND-A-HALF STOREY HOUSES

By building the roof a little higher at the ridge than on a one-storey house, and by building **dormer** windows out from the roof, extra space can be gained for additional bedrooms or a recreation room.

A one-and-a-half storey house.

TWO-STOREY HOUSES

The two-storey house has two full-size living areas under the same roof, making it the most economical style to build when you must have a large house. The kitchen, living room and dining room are usually downstairs, with several bedrooms and a bathroom upstairs. A two-storey house with a basement is a large house indeed, while the building lot may be small.

dormer: A window built upright in a sloping roof. Each dormer has its own small roof.

A two-storey house.

SPLIT-LEVEL HOUSES

The split-level design is the newest and most popular building style. Three or more living levels are arranged in either a front-to-back or side-to-side split arrangement. Bedrooms are usually on the upper level; kitchen, dining room and living room at ground level; and recreation room and utility room on the lower level. This style is particularly suited to a building lot that slopes. Six or more stair steps lead from one level to another.

It would be worthwhile for a building construction student to study a copy of his town's building **by-laws** and the subdivision map that goes with them. Both are available at the town clerk's office.

by-laws: A set of rules adopted by a town to control land use.

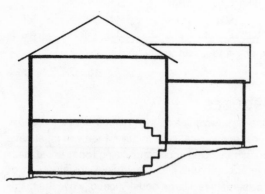

A split-level house on a side sloping lot.

A split-level house on a back sloping lot.

CHAPTER 2

Excavating
the Site
and Building
Footing Forms

WATCH FOR THESE WORDS

residential	diagonal
code	footing
lot	plumb
excavation	form
level	

HOW TO USE THESE WORDS

1. A **residential** building **lot** is marked out with steel stakes at all the corners.
2. You must follow the local building **code** when you are building a house.
3. The **excavation** for a house is often dug with a back hoe.
4. The **footing** for a house must be built **level**.
5. The corners of a building are square if the **diagonal** distances are equal.
6. The walls of a house should be **plumb**.
7. The **form** for a footing must be braced solidly in position.

FIND THE ANSWERS TO THESE QUESTIONS

1. List at least three things that might affect the position of the house on its building lot.
2. Describe two methods of accurately squaring the corners of a house layout.
3. What is the purpose of constructing batter boards?
4. Why are shallow saw cuts made in the batter boards where the lines pass over them?
5. What determines the amount of excavating needed for a house?
6. How is a plumb bob used to locate the building corners at the bottom of the excavation?
7. What tool is used to make sure the footing forms are built level?
8. Why must the footing forms be braced?
9. What is the purpose of a wall key?
10. What is used to prevent concrete from running out under the footing forms?

When the style of the house has been decided, the problem of positioning it on its building lot arises. Several points must be carefully considered. All **residential** areas have a building **code** that details such things as the minimum value of the house, the minimum distance from the front of the house to the property line, and the minimum amount of yard that must be left on each side.

residential: An area where people live or reside.

code: A set of rules or laws. The building code rules are called by-laws.

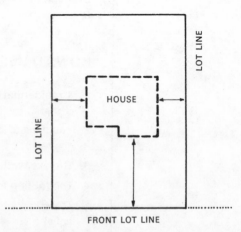

Local building codes set the minimum sizes of front and side yards.

Often, there are several well-shaped, healthy trees on the site that will greatly improve the appearance and value of the property if the house can be fitted in among them. If the neighbouring houses have established a line or pattern of placement, the house under construction should be located in a similar position so that it will not look out of place.

To lay out and stake the house position:

Once all restrictions have been taken into consideration, the actual laying out of the house may begin.

1. Drive 38 mm by 38 mm wooden stakes on both sides of the **lot** so that they show the intended location of the front of the house.

2. Measure back from the first two stakes along the sides of the lot a distance equal to the width of the house from front to back. Drive a stake at each of these points. Drive a nail in the centre of the top of these four stakes, and stretch heavy cords across the lot between the front stakes and between the back stakes.

lot: An area of land.

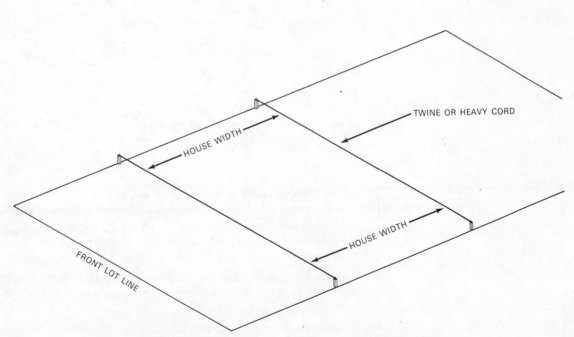

Establish the positions of the front and back of the house.

3. Measure in from one of the front stakes to locate the front corner of the house. Drive a stake here.

4. Measure along the line from this stake a distance equal to the length of the house and drive another stake.

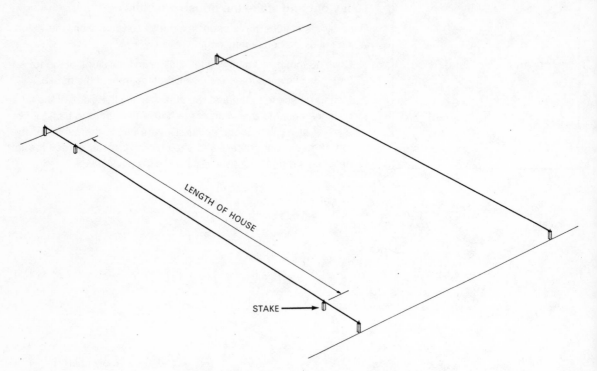

LENGTH OF HOUSE

STAKE →

Measure and stake the length of the house.

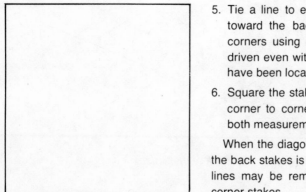

5. Tie a line to each of these corner stakes and stretch the lines toward the back line of the house. Roughly square the front corners using a framing square and attach the lines to stakes driven even with the back line. Now, all four corners of the house have been located.

6. Square the staked layout exactly by measuring the distance from corner to corner and then moving the back corner stakes until both measurements are equal.

When the diagonal distances are equal and the distance between the back stakes is equal to the distance between the front stakes, the lines may be removed and batter boards set up behind the four corner stakes.

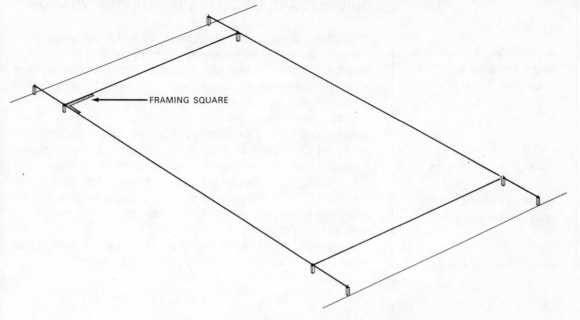

FRAMING SQUARE

Laying out the positions of the ends of the house.

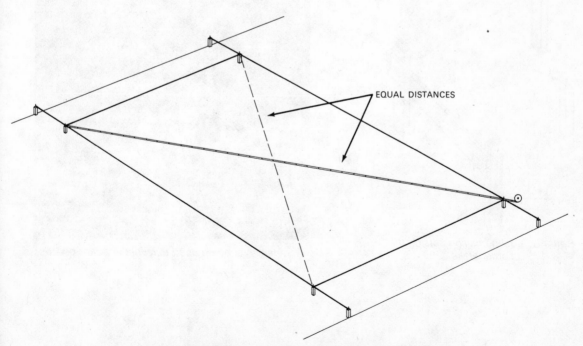

EQUAL DISTANCES

Measure the diagonals to make sure the layout is square.

excavation: A large hole dug in the ground, or the digging of the hole.

level: Horizontal. In line with the horizon.

BUILDING AND LOCATING THE BATTER BOARDS

The building corner stakes mark the exact length and width of the building, but they will be in the way during **excavation** and construction. Building batter boards and locating them solidly some distance away from the stakes provides a means of locating the corner points at any time after the stakes have been removed.

Batter boards are usually made of two pieces of 19 mm by 89 mm lumber nailed to three stakes to form a square corner. The stakes are lengths of 38 mm by 89 mm lumber, pointed and driven deeply into the earth about 1.5 m out from the building corner stakes.

The batter boards may be any height, but each must be level with the others. This levelling is usually done with a transit **level**. The job may be accomplished by using a long straight-edge, a carpenter's level and a series of stakes that are levelled one by one from one set of batter boards to the others. The straight-edge method is not usually accurate enough, especially with larger buildings.

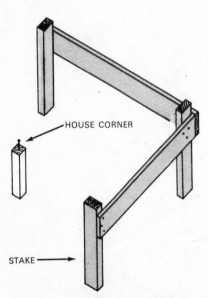

HOUSE CORNER

STAKE

Batter boards in position outside the corner stake.

A transit level being used to level the batter boards.

To fasten the building location lines:

When all four sets of batter boards are in place and levelled, the building location lines are fastened to them.

1. Stretch the front line directly over the corner stakes to the batter boards. Make shallow saw cuts in each board and tie the line in place through these cuts.

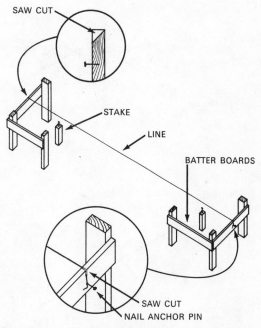

Lines are held firmly in position on the batter boards by saw cuts and anchor pins. The lines must be accurate and tight.

2. Run another line between the back batter boards, and accurately position them over the corner stakes. Check the position of this line at both ends by measuring from it to the saw cuts in the front batter boards. Both measurements should be the exact width of the house. Make saw cuts in the back boards and attach the line to them.

3. At one end of the house layout, stretch a line between the batter boards so that they cross the front and back lines directly over the corner stakes. To check the squareness of the corners further, measure 1.8 m from the point where the lines cross along the front line and 2.4 m along the end line. Make chalk marks on the lines at both points and measure the distance between them. This

diagonal distance should be 3.0 m. If it is not 3.0 m, move one end of the end line to correct the error. Make saw cuts in the batter boards, and attach both ends of the line to the batter boards.

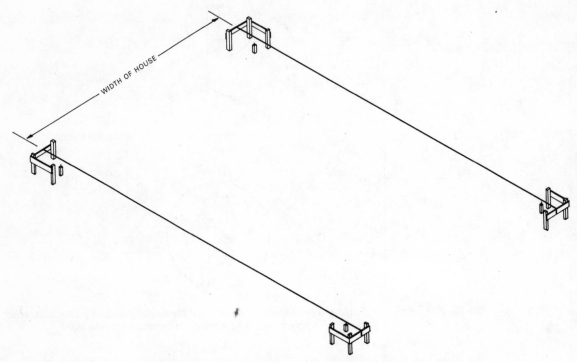

The distance between the lines is the exact width of the house.

diagonal: A line from one corner to the opposite corner of a square or rectangle.

4. Position a line between the batter boards at the other end of the lot layout. Check its position by measuring the length of the house from the saw cuts at the completed end. The building lines are now in place, and the **diagonal** distances from corner to corner of the layout should be equal. Make the saw cuts in the batter boards and secure the last line to them.

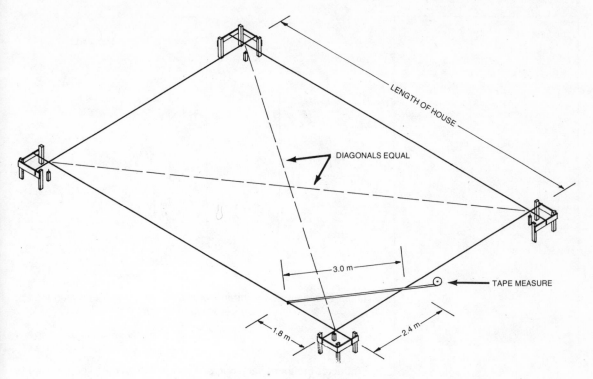

Two methods of making certain that the building layout has square corners.

EXCAVATING THE BUILDING SITE

The batter boards and lines outline the outer length and width of the house and show its exact position on the lot. They have been made level with each other so that measurements can be made from the line to the bottom of the excavation at any point. The excavator must be careful never to move these boards.

The type and depth of hole made for the building foundation depend on the house style and whether or not a basement is needed. Only a trench dug below the possible frost depth is required for a house without a basement; a basement under a split-level house may need to be excavated to two different depths.

The foundation wall must always rest on a wide, solid concrete slab called a **footing**. This footing must be wide enough to project beyond the foundation; the excavation must be sized accordingly.

footing: A concrete base which must be wide and thick enough to support the weight of the building.

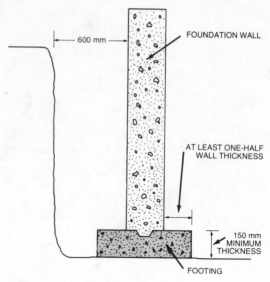

The local building code often states the size of the foundation footing on certain kinds of soil.

A tractor-mounted back hoe or a modern power shovel are used to do the digging. In the hands of a skilled operator, these machines can complete the excavation to the exact depth required and keep the sides fairly vertical. Very little hand shovelling is needed to level the bottom for the footings.

A power shovel being used to make a basement excavation.

BUILDING THE FORMS FOR THE FOOTINGS

plumb: Vertical. Exactly 90° to the horizon.

When the excavation has been completed, replace the lines on the batter boards and check them again for accuracy. Hang a **plumb** bob from each of the four intersection points so that its point almost touches the bottom of the excavation. Drive stakes at these points.

The four stakes mark the location of the foundation corners. The footing forms will be built around them. The distances from the batter board lines to the tops of the stakes should be equal.

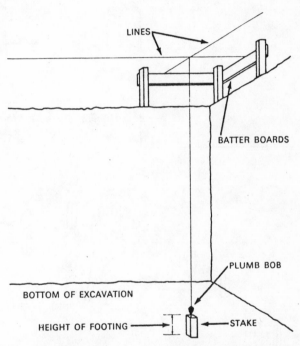

A plumb bob being used to locate the position of the foundation corners on the bottom of the excavation.

To build footing forms:

form: A mould made to hold concrete in position while it hardens.

1. Measure from the centre of each stake half of the wall thickness plus the thickness of the **form** material. For most house construction, this distance will be 125 mm plus 38 mm, or 163 mm. Drive stakes in the positions indicated in the drawing.

2. Stretch lines between these stakes as shown. Wrap the lines around the stakes and tie them. Drive stakes every 900 to 1200 mm along the outside of the lines so that the stakes just touch the lines.

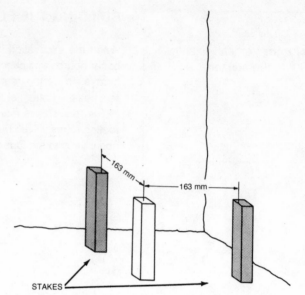

The first stakes for the outside footing form are driven half the wall thickness plus 38 mm outside the corner stake.

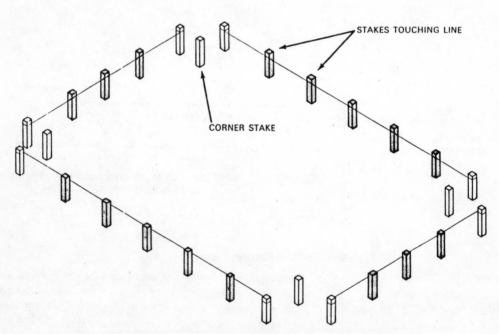

Tight lines speed the positioning of footing form stakes.

3. Position and nail lengths of 38 mm by 140 mm lumber to the stakes, making certain that all of the top edges are level and the same height as the corner stakes. Use a long carpenter's level. Note that if footings thicker than 140 mm are necessary, wider form material must be used.

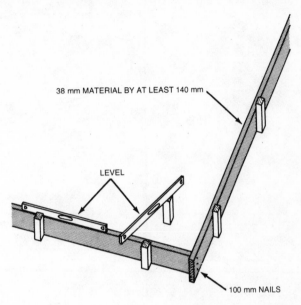

38 mm MATERIAL BY AT LEAST 140 mm

LEVEL

100 mm NAILS

Level the outside footing forms with the corner stakes.

4. When these outer footing forms are completed and levelled, measure from the inside face of the form the width of the footing plus one thickness of form material. For most house construction, this distance will be 500 mm, plus 38 mm, or 538 mm. Stretch a line from two end stakes and drive stakes to support the inside forms.

5. Position and nail straight 38 mm by 140 mm form material to these stakes. This inside footing form must be level with the outside form.

6. Cut lengths of 19 mm by 38 mm or larger material to the same length as the footing width and place them crosswise between the sides of the form. Drive stakes deeply into the ground about 300 mm away from both the inside and outside form sides. Cut and wedge pieces of 19 mm material against these stakes and nail the top ends to the footing form. The footing forms are now completed and braced against collapsing inwards or outwards. The inner braces are held in place by pressure from the outer braces and will be removed as the form is filled with concrete. The outer braces prevent the sides of the form from bulging from the weight of the concrete.

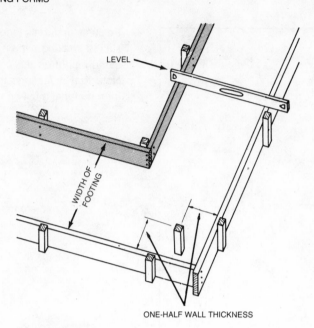

Build the inside forms level with the outside forms.

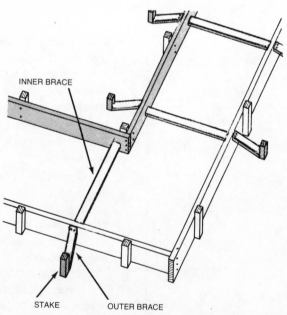

Footing forms should be solidly braced inside and out.

Forms should also be constructed at this time for the footings that will support the main-beam posts, the chimney or a fireplace. These footings must be wide enough to support the weight that will be placed on them. Typical footing forms are shown in the photograph and drawing.

Footing form for chimney or steel post.

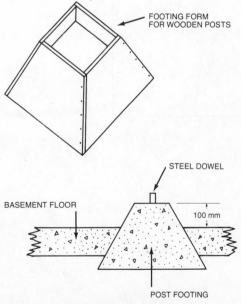

FOOTING FORM
FOR WOODEN POSTS

STEEL DOWEL

BASEMENT FLOOR

100 mm

POST FOOTING

Footing form for wooden post.

To prevent wet concrete from running out from under the footing forms, the outsides should be banked with earth.

In order to prevent the foundation wall from shifting on its footings from the pressure of earth against its outside surface, the footings are often formed with a groove cast into the top surface. This groove is called a **key** and should be located along the middle of the footing. A pattern of the key can be made by bevelling the edges of lengths of 38 mm by 89 mm lumber and suspending them in place on the footing forms. Straps are then nailed to the sides of the forms.

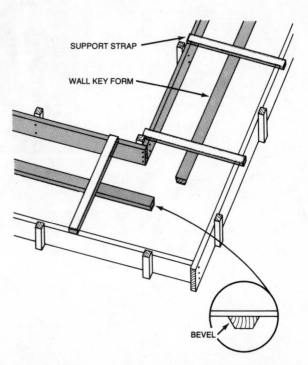

SUPPORT STRAP

WALL KEY FORM

BEVEL

An addition to the forms to make a wall key in the footing.

CHAPTER 3

Mixing Concrete and Pouring Footings

WATCH FOR THESE WORDS

aggregate	**alkali**
hydration	**silt**
acid	**concrete**

HOW TO USE THESE WORDS

1. Washed gravel or crushed stone is used as coarse **aggregate** in **concrete**.
2. The **hydration** of concrete continues as long as it is wet.
3. Water that has either too much **acid** or too much **alkali** is not good for making concrete.
4. The sand used in concrete should be clean and free of **silt**.

FIND THE ANSWERS TO THESE QUESTIONS

1. Name the materials used to make concrete.
2. Describe the method of storing cement.
3. What kind of water is best for making concrete?

4. What is the purpose of the silt test?

5. What is meant by describing a concrete mix as a 1: 2: 4 mix?

6. Find the amount of cement, sand and gravel needed for footings around a building 10 m long and 6 m wide if a 1: 2: 4 mix is used and the footings are 150 mm thick by 600 mm wide.

7. What does the screeding operation accomplish?

8. When may the footing forms be removed?

9. What is the purpose of weeping tile?

Concrete is a mixture of carefully measured portland cement, water, fine and course **aggregates**. The portland cement and water form a paste that completely surrounds the aggregate particles and hardens to bind them together in a solid rock-like mass.

Portland cement is manufactured by mixing limestone with certain amounts of clay or shale rock and burning the mixture in a blast furnace at a temperature of approximately 1000°C. When removed from the furnace, the heat-blended material is crushed and ground to a very fine powder. This is the finished portland cement. When portland cement is mixed with water, it first sets or stiffens and then hardens over a long period of time. The setting and hardening are caused by a chemical reaction between the cement and water called **hydration**. It is named portland cement because the colour of the hardened cement is much the same as the colour of the stone found in the rock quarries on the Isle of Portland, England.

Portland cement is sold in 40 kg bags. If a number of bags must be stored for some time, the storage area should be as dry as possible. The bags should be piled on a raised platform since the floor or the ground are too damp. When bagged cement is stored in piles for long periods of time, it tends to pack whether it is damp or not. Roll the bags on the floor to break up this packing. When you open a bag of cement, if you find it is full of lumps, squeeze some of them between your fingers. If the lumps crumble easily, the cement may be used, but if the lumps are hard, it is not likely to make good concrete.

Water used to make concrete should be clean and free of oil, **acid** or **alkali**. The manufacturers of portland cement advise using water that is fit to drink.

AGGREGATES

The sand and gravel for making concrete of lasting quality must be chosen as carefully as the water. They should be purchased from a reliable dealer who takes his materials from deposits that are known to make good concrete. A good sand for concrete will have particles ranging in size from very fine to 5 mm, while the coarse aggregate will be crushed stone or gravel with particles from 1.5 to 28 mm for thick footings and foundation walls. In walls, the largest particles

aggregate: A large number of pieces of material gathered together.

hydration: The combining of water and another substance in a definite proportion. This produces a compound. Heat is given off in the process.

acid: A liquid that gives water a sour taste when mixed with it. It combines with alkali to form salts.

alkali: A material also known as a base. It will cause water to have a bitter taste and make acids neutral.

silt: Fine particles of earth.

should not be more than one-fifth the thickness of the wall. There should be a uniform distribution of each size of particle from the smallest to the largest. For this reason, it is unlikely that aggregate taken directly from a gravel pit or stone crusher will make good concrete. It should first be passed through screens to separate the particle sizes. A screen with 5 mm openings will separate the fine aggregate from the coarse so that they may be mixed in the proper proportions.

If aggregates from well-known supplies are not available, there are tests to find out how usable an existing supply is. A **silt test** will show the amount of extremely fine material in the aggregate.

The silt test:

1. Fill an ordinary litre jar or bottle with the sand that is to be tested to a depth of 50 mm.
2. Add water until the jar is about three-quarters full.
3. Replace the top and shake the jar violently for a minute or two.
4. Allow it to stand for an hour. The silt, which is lighter in weight, will form a layer on top of the sand. If the silt layer is more than 3 mm thick, **do not** use the sand to make concrete. The sand may be washed and tested again to see if it is usable.

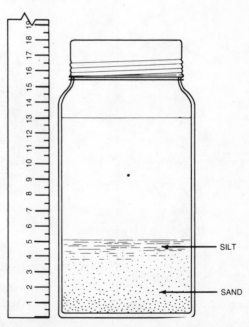

Measuring the silt content of a sand sample.

concrete: A mixture of cement, sand and gravel with water. Concrete hardens into a strong solid material.

MIXING CONCRETE

Concrete must be thoroughly mixed until its ingredients are evenly distributed. Mechanical mixers of many cubic capacities are available for the job.

Large businesses specialize in mixing concrete and delivering it to the building site in large truck-mounted mixers. They use high-quality materials and measure them carefully to make concrete in a variety of strengths.

Portable concrete mixers are available.

Truck-mounted mixers like this one can mix and deliver 4 or 5m³ of concrete in each load.

To mix concrete:

1. Pour about half of the mixing water into the mixer. The total amount of water used will depend on the wetness of the sand being used. If you are making a standard mix that calls for 23 L of water per bag of cement and the sand is wet, only 17.25 L should

be added. The other 5.75 L is already in the sand. A handful of dry sand feels dry; damp sand feels damp but will not squeeze into a ball as wet sand will. If the sand sparkles and wets your hand, it is very wet. The chart shows the amounts of water to use in two common concrete mixes. The mixer should be revolving while it is being filled.

AMOUNT OF WATER IF SAND IS DRY:	USE THIS MUCH WATER, IN LITRES, WHEN THE SAND IS:		
	Damp	Wet	Very Wet
19.5 L per bag of cement	17.25 L	15 L	13.75 L
23 L per bag of cement	18 L	17.25 L	15 L

Avoid using more water than this chart indicates to obtain maximum strength.

2. Shovel the correctly measured amounts of the fine and coarse aggregates into the mixer while gradually adding the cement and more of the water. The amount of each aggregate size used depends on the kind of job the concrete is intended for. For foundation walls and footings, a 1:2:4 mix is commonly used. This means that with one bag of portland cement you will mix twice that amount of sand and four times that amount of gravel. The large amount of coarse aggregate fills the forms quickly while the sand and cement fill the spaces between the heavy particles to bind them together.

To mix 1 m³ of concrete, you will use 8 bags of cement, 0.43 m³ of sand, and 0.86 m³ of gravel or crushed stone. The cement and sand fill the spaces between the particles of gravel or crushed stone. The amount of each material needed to fill all of a footing form may be found by multiplying the thickness of the footing by its width and by its total length. This gives the number of cubic metres of concrete needed. Then multiply this figure by the amounts of material in 1 m³ of concrete.

Example:

Requirements for a 150 mm by 600 mm footing for a house that is 8 m wide and 12 m long.

Thickness of footing = 150 mm = 0.15 m

Width of footing = 600 mm = 0.6 m

Total length of footing = 8 + 8 + 12 + 12 = 40 m

Amount of concrete needed = 0.15 × 0.6 × 40 = 3.6 m^3

Amount of cement needed = 3.6 × 8 = 28.8 or 29 bags

Amount of sand needed = 3.6 × 0.43 = 1.5 m^3

Amount of gravel needed = 3.6 × 0.86 = 3 m^3

When loading the mixer, the worker must count the number of shovelfuls of each material added. The number of shovels needed to equal one bag of cement may be found by constructing a bottomless wooden box with sides measuring 300 mm and counting the number of shovels needed to fill it level.

3. Keep about 10% of the water until all of the solid materials have been placed in the mixer. Add this water and allow the mixer to run for one minute per cubic metre of concrete in the mixer. The concrete should be poured into the forms as soon as possible after mixing. If it has been left for about 45 min, it must be mixed again because it will have begun to set. Do not add more water while remixing, since this will weaken the concrete.

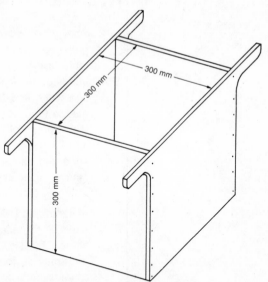

A simple box for measuring the amount of aggregate equal to one bag of portland cement.

To mix concrete using Imperial measure:

1. Pour about half of the mixing water into the mixer. Again, the total amount of water used will depend on the wetness of the sand being used. If you are making a standard mix that calls for 5 gal. of water per bag of cement and the sand is wet, only 3¾ gal. should be added. The other 1¼ gal. is already in the sand. The chart shows the amounts of water to use in two common concrete mixes. The mixer should be revolving while it is being filled.

2. Shovel the correctly measured amounts of the fine and coarse aggregates into the mixer while gradually adding the cement and more of the water. For foundation walls and footings, a 1:2:4 mix is commonly used. This means that with one bag of portland cement, you will mix 2 ft.^{3} of sand and 4 ft.^{3} of gravel.

To mix 1 yd.^{3} of concrete, you will use 6 bags of cement, 12 ft.^{3} of sand, and 24 ft.^{3} of gravel or crushed stone. The cement and sand fill the spaces between the particles of gravel or crushed stone resulting in 27 ft.^{3} of concrete. The amount of each material needed to fill all of a footing form may be found by multiplying the thickness of the footing by its width and by its total length, which gives the number of cubic yards of concrete needed. Then multiply this figure by the amounts of material in 1 yd.^{3} of concrete.

AMOUNT OF WATER IF SAND IS DRY:	USE THIS MUCH WATER, IN GALLONS, WHEN THE SAND IS:		
	Damp	Wet	Very Wet
4¼ gal. per bag of cement	3¾ gal.	3¼ gal.	3 gal.
5 gal. per bag of cement	4½ gal.	3¾ gal.	3¼ gal.

Avoid using more water than this chart indicates to obtain maximum strength.

Example:

Requirements for a 6 in. by 24 in. footing for a house that is 20 ft. wide and 32 ft. long.

Thickness of footing = 6 in. = $1/2$ ft.

Width of footing = 24 in. = 2 ft.

Total length of footing = 20 + 20 + 32 + 32 = 104 ft.

Amount of concrete needed $= 1/2 \times 2 \times 104 = 104$ ft.^{3}
27 ft.^{3} = 1 yd.^{3}, therefore
104 ft.^{3} $= {}^{104}/_{27} \simeq 4$ yd.^{3}

Amount of cement needed = $4 \times 6 = 24$ bags

Amount of sand needed = $4 \times 12 = 48$ ft.^{3} = $1^{3}/_{4}$ yd.^{3}

Amount of gravel needed = $4 \times 24 = 96$ ft.^{3} = $3^{1}/_{2}$ yd.^{3}

When loading the mixer, the workman must again count the number of shovelfuls of each material. The number of shovels needed to equal 1 ft.^{3} may be found by constructing a bottomless wooden box measuring one foot square and counting the number of shovelfuls needed to fill it level.

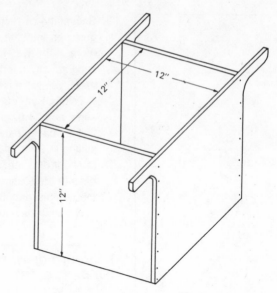

A simple box for measuring 1 ft³ of aggregate.

POURING CONCRETE INTO FOOTING FORMS

The concrete is moved from the mixer to the forms in metal boxed wheelbarrows and dumped into the form by lifting the handles of the wheelbarrow. Pour the concrete where it is needed in the form. Do not drag it into position with a hoe or shovel because this tends to separate the coarse particles from the fine ones.

Tamp the concrete along the edges of the form with a hoe, or lightly spade it along the edges to remove air bubbles and move the coarse particles away from the outside for a smoother finish. A length of 38 mm lumber makes a good tamper. Remove the inner form braces as you come to them.

A worker using a hoe to tamp freshly placed concrete.

As the footing form is filled with concrete, it should be **struck off** level with the top edges by resting a straight length of 38 mm lumber edgewise on the surface, pressing it down and moving it in a sawing motion along the forms. A small amount of concrete should be kept ahead of the straight-edge to fill in the low spots in the surface.

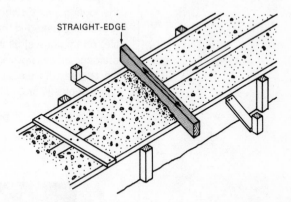

Move the straight-edge along the forms with a sawing motion.

This striking off operation is also known as **screeding** or **rodding**; in the case of wall footings, this is often the only surface finishing carried out. For a better surface finish, the concrete is allowed to begin to set. When all of the surface water is gone, a wooden float is used to make a better finish on the surface and correct any flaws left by the screeding operation. The float is used with its bottom surface held perfectly flat to prevent the edges from digging in. A metal trowel may be used for a particularly smooth finish. Both tools are shown in the drawing. Too much floating or trowelling brings cement to the surface and weakens the concrete.

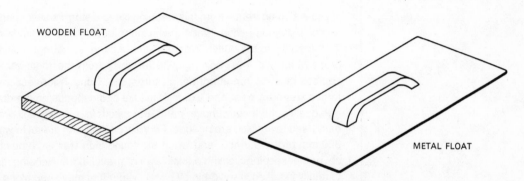

Examples of wood and steel floats.

For concrete to harden completely and reach its maximum strength, it should be kept wet. As soon as there is no water to hydrate the cement, all hardening ceases. Foundation footings should be covered with burlap and wetted by sprinkling over a ten day period. The wood forms may be removed two or three days after pouring, but care must be taken to prevent damaging the concrete.

When the footing forms have been removed, level the area outside the footings with a shovel, and cover it with about 50 mm of coarse gravel or crushed stone. String a row of **clay drainage tile** (weeping tile) on this gravel all the way around the excavation so that a slight drainage slope is provided. Cover the tops of the joints in the weeping tile course with pieces of asphalt building paper. There are several types of plastic drain pipe that may be used instead of clay tile.

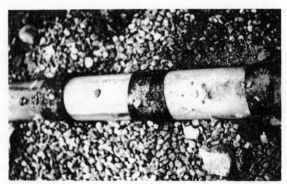

Cover the joints in the weeping tile course with building paper.

Dig a sloping trench from this weeping tile to a storm sewer connection or a drainage ditch. Place gravel in the trench, and lay tile from a T-shaped tile to the outlet. Where neither a storm sewer nor a ditch is present, the tile must be run quite far away from the footings, and courses must be run at right angles from the X and T-connections to form a **weeping bed.** The extent of the tile bed depends on the drainage quality of the surrounding earth. For example, a sandy soil drains easily and fewer tiles are needed. Fill the trenches with gravel to within 300 mm of the surface, and when the foundation wall is completed, cover the weeping tile with a thick layer of gravel. If the weeping tile is carefully installed, it will drain off all rain water that may seep along the foundation wall and footings.

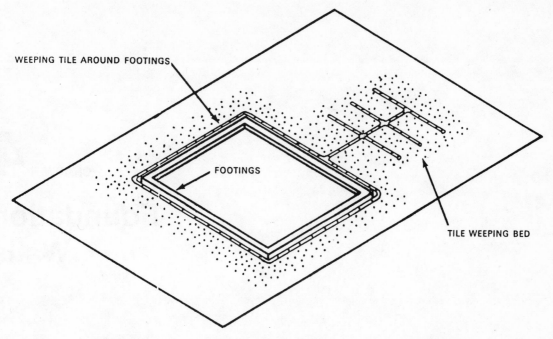

WEEPING TILE AROUND FOOTINGS

FOOTINGS

TILE WEEPING BED

A drainage system of clay weeping tile for foundation walls and footings.

To prepare to pour the basement floor, clean up the excavation bottom by removing all scrap wood and parts of the footing forms. Level off any high spots with a shovel and spread an even 150 mm layer of gravel or crushed stone over the floor area to within 50 mm of the top of the footings.

Gravel underlay for the basement floor slab.

CHAPTER 4

Foundation Walls

POURED CONCRETE WALLS

WATCH FOR THESE WORDS

seepage
sheathing
salvage
straps

wallings
basement
bevel

HOW TO USE THESE WORDS

1. The **seepage** of water through foundation walls will make the basement damp.
2. Builders try to **salvage** the **sheathing** lumber used to build concrete forms.
3. Wooden **straps** help to hold wall forms in place.
4. **Wallings** help to brace the forms for poured concrete walls.
5. **Basement** walls are usually made of concrete.
6. The edges of a piece of wood may be cut to a **bevel** shape.

FIND THE ANSWERS TO THESE QUESTIONS

1. What are the disadvantages of using lumber sheathed forms for pouring concrete walls?
2. How are plywood form sections held the correct distance apart?
3. Why is it good practice to oil the form sections?
4. Why is it necessary to brace the sides of door-opening forms?
5. How may the wall form be checked for straightness?
6. When should the sill anchor bolts be set in place?
7. How long should the forms be left in place after the concrete has been poured?
8. Describe the correct method of filling the wall forms.

When the concrete footings have hardened for several days and the forms have been removed, construction of the foundation walls may begin. If the footings have been carefully levelled, your work will be much easier.

Foundation walls in house construction are of two types. The poured concrete wall is preferred by many builders because of its great strength and greater resistance to water **seepage**. The concrete block wall, which is less expensive and much faster to complete, is in popular use on well-drained building lots. Both types of foundation wall will be described in this chapter.

BUILDING THE FORMS FOR A POURED CONCRETE WALL

Before the development of waterproof glues for the manufacture of plywood, the forms for poured concrete foundations were framed with 38 mm by 89 mm studs and sheathed with horizontally nailed boards. The **sheathing** was often square-edged but ship-lap or tongue-and-groove edge matched boards were used where a smoother wall was desired.

When the concrete was poured and had hardened, the forms were torn down. In the process, much of the wood material was ruined for further use. This, of course, added to the cost of the building. Any wood the builder managed to **salvage** from the wall forms had to be cleaned before he could use it in the framing and sheathing of the house. The whole process, as you can imagine, was costly and wasted time. The drawing shows the construction of a lumber sheathed wall form.

seepage: Water leaking through very small cracks or holes.

sheathing: The material used to cover a frame.

salvage: To save materials used in one job for later use in another job.

Waterproof plywood glues have made great time savings possible in the construction of wall forms. They have made it possible for masonry workers to make up sets of framed panels in standard wall heights and various widths. These plywood panels have proven to be long-wearing and economical for a large number of construction jobs. They also make a much smoother wall than lumber forms.

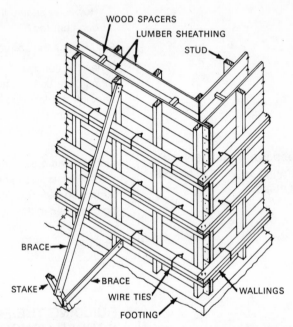

A lumber sheathed form for a poured concrete wall. The ties are twisted inside the form to tighten them.

The standard height of a basement wall is 2400 mm, which is also the length of a standard sheet of plywood. When the plywood is laid on its side, its 1200 mm width is often large enough for foundations under houses that do not have a basement. By sawing 2400 mm sheets into widths of 300 mm, 600 mm, and 900 mm, walls of any length or height may be formed. The illustration shows the method of framing plywood form sections. The holes in the panels and the notches on their edges are used for the placement of wire ties to hold the panels in place.

This method of building foundation forms is so commonly used that special wire ties and wedges are manufactured to make the job even easier. The ties also act as spacers to hold the form sections apart to the exact thickness of the wall.

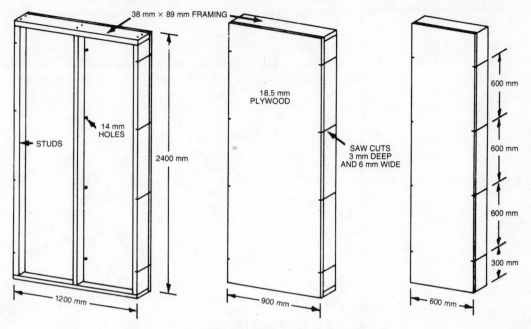

38 mm × 89 mm FRAMING

STUDS

14 mm HOLES

2400 mm

1200 mm

18.5 mm PLYWOOD

SAW CUTS 3 mm DEEP AND 6 mm WIDE

900 mm

600 mm

600 mm

600 mm

300 mm

600 mm

Plywood form sections are built up in several widths.

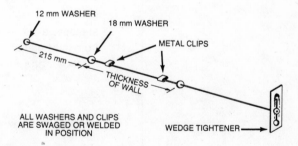

12 mm WASHER

18 mm WASHER

METAL CLIPS

215 mm

THICKNESS OF WALL

ALL WASHERS AND CLIPS ARE SWAGED OR WELDED IN POSITION

WEDGE TIGHTENER

One style of manufactured wire form tie with its wedge.

Masonry contractors may use steel framed plywood form panels which can be purchased with special hardware for locking them in place.

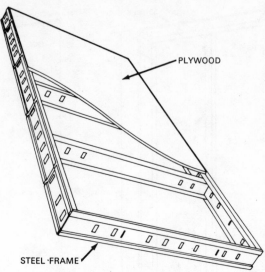

Steel framed plywood form sections are more rigid and have a longer life than the wood framed style.

To erect a wall form:

1. To begin installing plywood sections for foundation walls, locate the exact outside corners of the foundation by hanging a plumb bob from the point where the batter board lines cross. Mark the locations with chalk and stretch a chalk line along the footing from one mark to the other. **Snap** the line to mark the position of the outer wall form. A tightly stretched chalk line is snapped by lifting it near its mid-point and letting it fall. When the line snaps against the footing, it deposits some chalk in a straight line along its length.

2. Measure a distance equal to the thickness of the foundation wall from this outer chalk line, and again use this chalk line to mark the location of the inner forms.

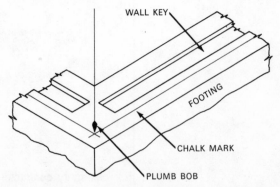

Using a plumb bob and chalk line to locate and mark the wall position on the footing.

3. Brush a coating of lubricating oil onto the flat surface of each form section. The oil will make it much easier to remove the forms from the poured wall and will also keep the form boards from absorbing water from the concrete.

4. Position and temporarily brace the inside wall forms so that they line up along the inner chalk line. The wire ties must be placed in their notches as the sections are butted together. Align the faces of the sections and fasten them together at top and bottom with nails driven through the adjoining studs.

5. Insert wire ties through the 14 mm holes in the form sections and place one outside form section in position at a time. The wire ties may be poked through the holes in these sections more easily if the bottom of the section is placed on the chalk line and the top is leaned some distance out. Gradually raise the section into position while another worker guides the ties, beginning with the lower one and working up.

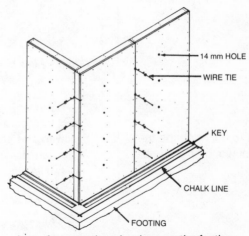

14 mm HOLE

WIRE TIE

KEY

CHALK LINE

FOOTING

Inner form sections in place on the footing.

straps: Narrow strips of wood.

wallings: Lengths of lumber used as straps or supports across the face of the framework.

basement: The part of a building that is entirely or partly below ground level.

6. Carefully align the faces of the outer form sections and nail them together. Do not drive these nails in all the way. This will allow you to remove them easily when taking down the forms. **Straps** nailed across the tops of the form sections will keep them from tipping until the **wallings** and braces are installed.

7. Position the **basement** window frames between the form sections where shown on the building blueprint, and fasten them to the forms with nails driven through the plywood. The top of a basement window frame is usually level with the top of the foundation wall. If the wall is thicker than the depth of the window frame, an extension must be made and fastened to the frame with a few nails as shown. The extension is always placed against the outside wall form.

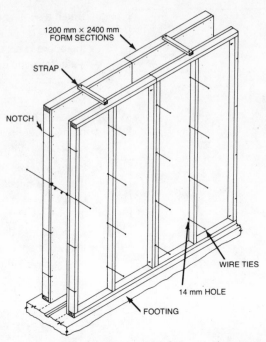

1200 mm × 2400 mm
FORM SECTIONS

STRAP

NOTCH

WIRE TIES

14 mm HOLE

FOOTING

The wire ties must be installed as the form sections are placed.
Fasten the sections together with nails.

Basement door-opening forms should also be placed in the correct location and nailed in place. Doorway forms and large window frames should be well-braced to prevent the weight of wet concrete from bowing the sides of the frame. **Bevel** cut the edges of two lengths of 38 mm by 89 mm lumber and fasten them to the

bevel: To cut or shape the edges of wood on a slant.

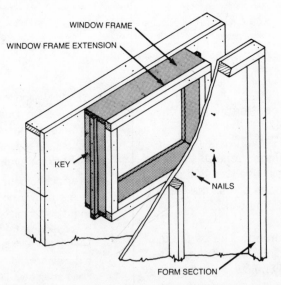

WINDOW FRAME

WINDOW FRAME EXTENSION

KEY

NAILS

FORM SECTION

A window frame positioned and fastened to the forms.

outer sides of the door-opening form with a few nails. When the form is removed, this **nailing key** remains locked in the concrete to provide a surface for fastening the door frame to the wall.

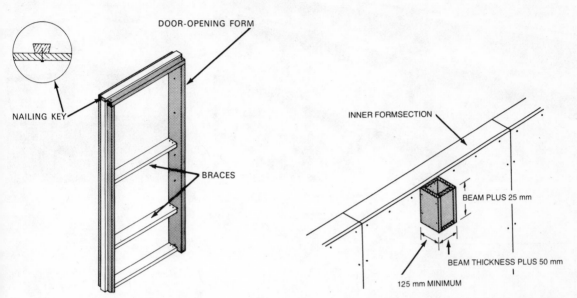

The construction and bracing of a door-opening form. *The construction and placement of a beam pocket form.*

8. If the blueprint shows the main support beam of the house resting in pockets in the top of the foundation wall, two box forms will have to be built and nailed to the inside wall form in the correct position. The pockets are usually in the middle of the end walls.

9. Select long, straight lengths of 38 mm by 89 mm lumber for use as wallings and toenail them to the form studs above and below the wire ties. Place the wedge tighteners over the ends of the ties and drive them down to push the form sections tightly against the large washers on the ties.

10. Stretch a building line along each wall from corner to corner and brace the forms where needed to hold them perfectly straight with the line. If there is not enough room around the outside of the forms for such bracing, install the braces against the sides of the excavation or against stakes driven outside the excavation. When the inside and outside form sections have been straightened and braced, the wall form is ready to be filled with concrete.

The wallings make the wall forms very rigid.

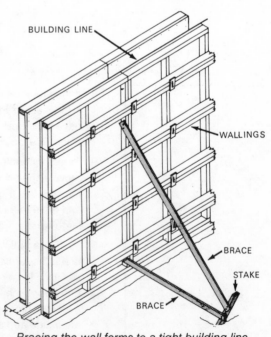

Bracing the wall forms to a tight building line.

POURING THE FOUNDATION WALL

The whole foundation wall should be poured during one working day in order to make the strongest and most waterproof wall that is free from joints.

Use the same amounts of water and dry materials in each batch of concrete, so that each batch will be the same. A fairly stiff mix makes a stronger wall than a sloppy mix; the coarse aggregate will not settle to the bottom if the mix is stiff.

Pour the concrete into the form in layers 150 to 250 mm thick. Work each layer thoroughly with a long-handled shovel or length of lumber to remove air pockets, and compact the concrete. A movable plank or plywood ramp against the top of the wall form allows the wheelbarrow to be positioned for pouring. Carefully work the concrete under the window forms to remove any large air pockets which will result in hollow spaces when the concrete hardens.

As soon as the wall form is full, strike the surface level with the top of the form and then use a float to smooth any rough areas. After the concrete has begun to set but before it hardens, the anchor bolts for the sill plate must be set in place. Push 12 mm diameter bolts into the concrete, leaving 50 mm or more of each bolt above the surface. Press the surrounding concrete tightly against each bolt, making sure each bolt is vertical and the same distance from the inside edge of the wall as the others. These bolts should be spaced 1200 to 1800 mm apart.

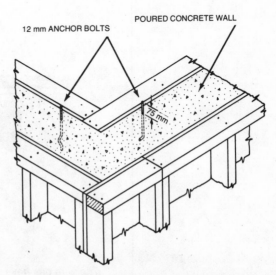

12 mm ANCHOR BOLTS

POURED CONCRETE WALL

75 mm

The anchor bolts should be pushed 150 mm into the concrete.

The wall forms should be left in place for two days or more and then carefully removed and cleaned. The wire ties are usually made so that they break off easily behind the large washer when the wire is bent.

A poured concrete wall when the forms are removed. Note the wire tie ends.

The illustration shows the wall with the ends of the ties removed.

The wire ties have been broken off leaving very little roughness.

CONCRETE BLOCK WALLS

WATCH FOR THESE WORDS

cinders	precast
insulation	reinforce
hydrated	mesh
score	caulking
fibrous	parging
corrugated	debris

HOW TO USE THESE WORDS

1. **Cinder** blocks provide better **insulation** than concrete blocks.
2. One of the materials used to make mortar is **hydrated** lime.
3. A wide chisel called a bolster is used to **score** and cut concrete blocks.
4. **Caulking** and **fibrous** damp proofing are both used where water must be sealed out.
5. Wooden door frames are held in place with **corrugated** metal strips.
6. Some parts of block walls may be **precast** and placed into position as the wall is built.
7. Concrete may be **reinforced** with steel rods or wire.
8. Wire **mesh** is often used to tie block walls together.
9. Cement **parging** helps to seal the outside of block walls.
10. Do not allow building **debris** to get mixed into fresh concrete.

FIND THE ANSWERS TO THESE QUESTIONS

1. What is the difference in the materials used to make heavy and light concrete blocks?
2. Name five styles of concrete blocks.
3. Describe the correct way to store concrete blocks on the job.
4. What materials are used in the mixing of mortar?
5. What is the purpose of laying a dry course of blocks on the footing?
6. How is a storey pole used in the building of the leads?
7. What is the purpose of tooling the mortar joints?
8. What is a closure block?
9. How are window frames fastened rigidly to the block wall?

cinders: Ashes and pieces of partly burned coal.

insulation: Protection against heat or cold.

10. Describe the correct method of tying a non-load bearing partition to the main foundation wall.

11. What is the purpose of the parging operation?

12. Why should the wall be dampened just before parging?

13. Describe two methods of putting a decorative finish on parging above ground level.

14. What is the minimum thickness of basement floors in house construction?

15. Why should the surface of a concrete floor be floated before trowelling?

CONCRETE BLOCK FOUNDATIONS

The concrete blocks used in building foundation walls may be the heavy type made of cement, sand and crushed stone, or the lighter cinder block that is made using coal cinders in place of the crushed stone. The heavy blocks have sharper edges which give a better appearance. However, the light **cinder** blocks give much more **insulation** against heat and cold.

Concrete blocks are made in many specialized shapes and sizes. A few of these different styles are shown here. The size of a stretcher block is 190 mm high and 390 mm long. There are five standard widths: 90 mm, 140 mm, 190 mm, 240 mm, and 290 mm. When the standard mortar thickness of 10 mm is added, each block course measures 200 mm in height.

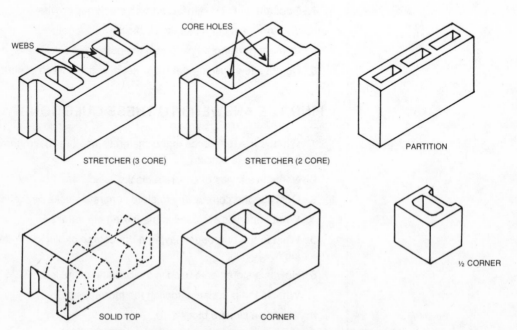

Some of the many shapes and sizes of concrete blocks.

hydrated: Combined with water.

Concrete blocks should be stored off the ground on raised platforms and should be covered to keep them from getting wet. Do not wet the blocks before laying them.

The material used to bond the blocks together into a solid wall is called **mortar**. This mortar is a mixture of one part masonry cement to three parts mortar sand with just enough water to make a workable mortar that will stick to the trowel and blocks. Masonry cement is basically portland cement with a measured amount of **hydrated** lime added to make the cement easier to work. The sand is especially graded for masonry use.

Mortar should be mixed in a mechanical mixer to ensure the best possible results. It may also be mixed in a mortar box by first mixing the dry sand and cement with a mortar hoe, then pulling the mix to one end of the box and gradually dragging it into a measured amount of water which has been poured at the other end.

Locate the corners of the foundation on the footings using the plumb bob and building lines, and mark the wall locations on the footings with a chalk line. Place mortar boards along the footing, spaced 1200 to 1500 mm apart, just behind the place where the workers will stand. Pile a number of concrete blocks between each mortar board. The illustration shows the position of mortar boards on a scaffold. The task of one worker is to place mortar on the boards and pile blocks between them.

Mortar boards positioned on a scaffold within easy reach of workers.

To build the leads:

The corners are built up five or six courses ahead of the middle part of each wall. These corners are called **leads**.

1. Beginning at one corner, set a course of blocks in place on the footing with the outside edges of the blocks even with the chalk line. Space the blocks 10 mm apart and do not use mortar. Slightly

widen or narrow each space by an equal amount until a half or whole block fits exactly at the end of the course. The spacing between each block should be no narrower than 8 mm and no wider than 12 mm. This spacing will be the end mortar joint size for the whole wall.

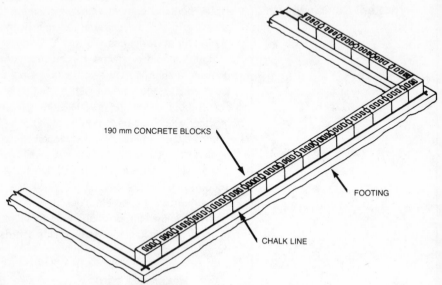

190 mm CONCRETE BLOCKS

FOOTING

CHALK LINE

Laying out the block spacing with a dry course.

score: To cut lightly with a bolster. Each score mark looks like a straight scratch.

If this slight adjustment in spacing does not achieve the desired result, the mason must cut a block at one end to shorten the course. To achieve a straight cut, **score** the block on both sides and cut it with a brick bolster and hammer.

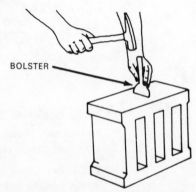

BOLSTER

Using a brick bolster and hammer to cut a concrete block.

Concrete blocks may also be cut with special power masonry saws. These circular-bladed saws do the job more easily and accurately, but you must **remember to wear protective glasses and a face mask**, particularly when sawing indoors. The face mask will keep you from breathing in sawdust (silica powder) which is very harmful to your lungs.

This dry course procedure should be followed on each of the walls. Mark the footing at the right-hand end of each block. Lift the blocks off the footing, and place them on end for mortaring.

2. Mix a quantity of mortar. Place one or two shovelfuls of mortar on each mortar board. Using a trowel, spread mortar on the footing for the first corner block. Furrow the mortar as shown.

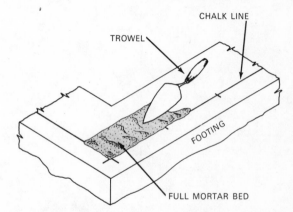

Using a trowel to furrow the mortar bed for the corner block.

3. Set the corner block on the mortar, and carefully align it with both chalk lines. The thick side of the block webs should be facing up to make a wider base for the mortar for the next course. Place a level across the top of the block; push down lightly on the block to bed it in the mortar. Use the handle of the trowel to tap the block into level position. Place a level lengthwise on the block to make sure that it is in fact level. Adjust it if necessary.

4. Spread and furrow mortar for the next block. Butter one end of a stretcher block and using both hands, lift the block and place it gently against the corner block. Carefully push the block down into position, leaving the correct thickness of mortar joint between the blocks. Use the level and trowel to adjust the position of the block and remove the excess mortar that is pushed out between and under the blocks.

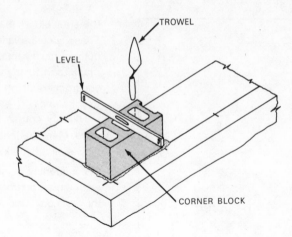

Levelling the corner block using the trowel handle.

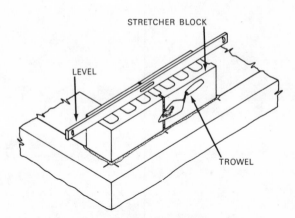

Removing excess mortar with the trowel.

5. Spread mortar and place two more blocks along the wall and three blocks along the adjacent wall footing. Carefully position and level each block and remove excess mortar. Check the alignment of the blocks with the level used as a straight-edge.

6. As the next courses are laid, mortar is spread only on the top outer edges of the blocks. Each block overlaps the blocks below it exactly halfway.

   When building walls with blocks wider than 190 mm, special corner blocks are used. The small end of these blocks is the same size as the end of a 190 mm block.

7. Make sure to check each block with a level as it is laid. Use the level vertically to check both sides of the corner.

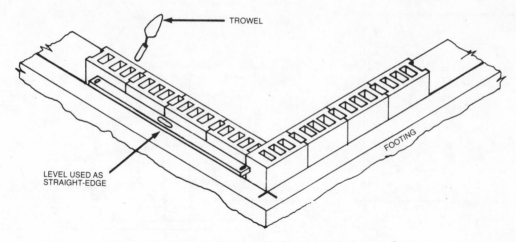

Aligning the blocks with a level held against their outer faces.

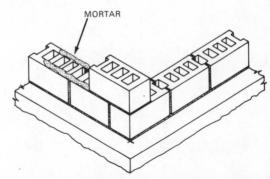

Spread mortar only on the outer top surfaces of the blocks.

The shape of corner block used in walls thicker than 190 mm.

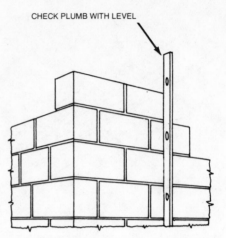

CHECK PLUMB WITH LEVEL

Make sure that the wall is vertical.

A storey pole marked every 200 mm makes accurate location of the top of each course a simple matter. A storey pole can be made from a 2400 mm length of 19 mm lumber.

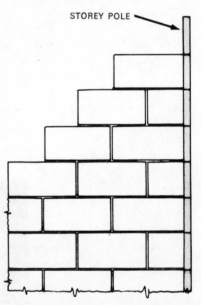

STOREY POLE

Rest the storey pole on the footing to check the height of each block course.

The finished leads at one corner are shown here. Similar leads are also built at all the other corners. Once the leads have been built, work may begin on the centre section of each wall.

Completed leads at one corner of a foundation.

Before the mortar has time to harden, all of the joints should be made concave (tooled) with a tool made for this purpose. The tool may be made from 16 mm diameter tubing or may be purchased in an "S" shape. Tooling compresses the surface of the mortar to make a more watertight joint. Tool the horizontal joints first, then tool the vertical ones.

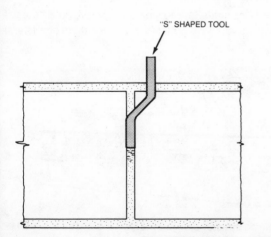

"S" SHAPED TOOL

TOOL MADE FROM 16 mm TUBING

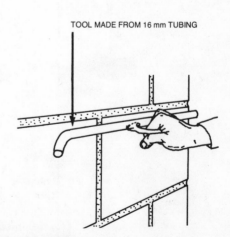

Two styles of tools used to tool the mortar joints.

To fill in between the leads:

1. Stretch a line from corner to corner at the top edge of the first course of blocks. The line aids in positioning and levelling each block and makes certain that the block course is straight. The first course between the leads should be laid in a full bed of mortar and spaced according to the marks established by the dry course. If two people work in from each end of a wall, the job is easier and faster.

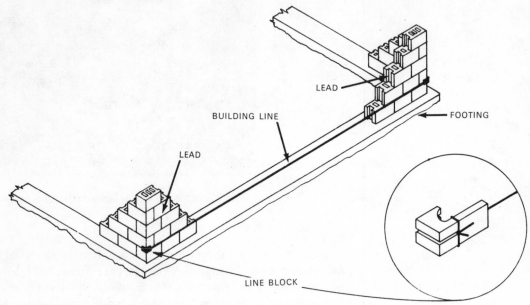

Attaching a building line to the leads as a guide to keep each course level and straight.

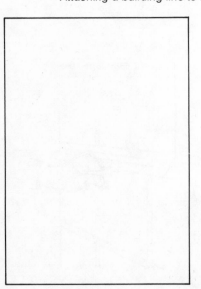

2. For greater speed, stand two or three blocks on end and butter them all at the same time. Spread mortar on the previous course for as many blocks as you have buttered and place them one after the other.

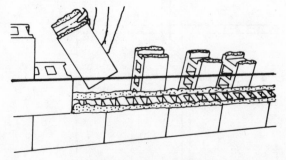

Spreading mortar on several blocks at a time increases the worker's speed.

3. To lay the centre or **closure** block in each course, both ends of the closure block and the ends of the blocks next to it must be buttered. The closure block is then carefully lowered into the opening and levelled.

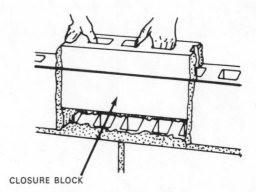

CLOSURE BLOCK

Placing the closure block.

4. When courses of blocks have been built up to the tops of the leads, build the corners up to the finished wall height, thus forming new leads. A foundation wall enclosing a basement usually has eleven or twelve block courses to make a height of either 2200 mm or 2400 mm.

New leads are built on top of the others to build the upper wall.

5. Cut strips of **fibrous** damp coursing material to cover the core holes of the previous courses before laying any of the blocks in the top course. Fibrous damp coursing is a plastic material that has a shiny surface on one side and a dull surface on the other. It is usually purchased in a roll. Place the shiny side down over the core holes. This material prevents ground water from soaking up through the wall into the wood framing of the house.

fibrous: Filled with threads of some material which gives additional strength.

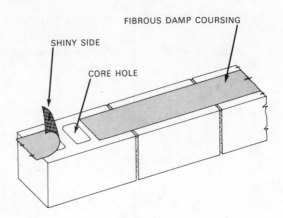

Fibrous damp coursing being installed under the top course of blocks.

6. The top course of blocks should be of the solid top style, and the end spaces should be filled with mortar. Set a 12 mm diameter anchor bolt in every fourth end joint, 38 to 50 mm from the inside edge of the wall. If you use the regular stretcher blocks, the core holes should be filled with mortar to make a surface with a flat top.

Sill anchor bolts are set into the mortar joints in the top course.

INSTALLING A DOOR FRAME IN A BLOCK WALL

Door frames may be purchased assembled and braced, or in pieces ready to put together. Place the frame in position on the footing and block it up to the correct height with pieces of wood. If a precast concrete sill is being used, it should be set in place with mortar. The door frame may then be fitted to the sill. Door frames in partition walls should be blocked so that they will sit on the concrete floor when it is poured. Brace the frame in a true vertical position and build the wall.

A door frame braced in a vertical position in a partition wall.

The blocks laid against the door frame may be square-ended corner blocks, bullnosed corner or sash blocks, or square-ended sash blocks.

Fasten a **corrugated** metal tie to the door frame at every third mortar joint beginning at the top of the first course. Fill the block cores beneath and above the ties with mortar.

The **lintel** (the horizontal piece of wood or concrete that supports the structure above a window or door opening) above the door frame is often made of poured concrete. Build a form and fill it with a 1: 2: 3 concrete mix. Two 12 mm steel rods should be placed in the middle of the lintel space 100 mm apart and running the full length of the lintel. Lintel blocks and **precast** concrete lintels are also available.

corrugated: Bent into wrinkles which are the same size and shape.

precast: Made up in a form for later use.

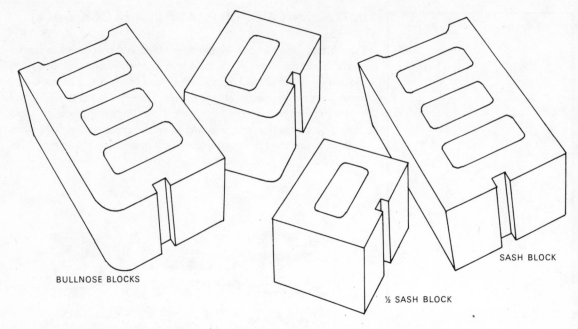

BULLNOSE BLOCKS

½ SASH BLOCK

SASH BLOCK

Styles of blocks used next to the window and door frames.

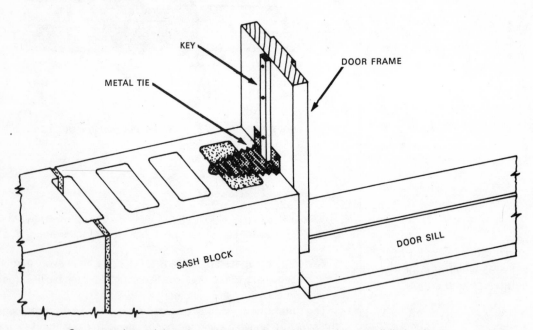

KEY

METAL TIE

DOOR FRAME

SASH BLOCK

DOOR SILL

Corrugated metal ties plus a key strip hold the door frame solidly in place.

A simply constructed form used to mould a poured concrete door lintel.

INSTALLING A BASEMENT WINDOW AND FRAME

Basement windows in block walls are prepared and placed in much the same way as the door frames. When most of the wall will be below ground level, the windows are positioned with their top surfaces even with the top of the last block course. Drive two 60 mm nails partway into the window sash at each mortar joint to help hold the frame rigid, or use sheet metal ties.

With these small, high windows, solid top or filled blocks are used for a sill. A slope is formed on the sill with a layer of cement plaster trowelled on at the same time as the wall is coated with plaster.

Larger windows are usually fitted with precast concrete sills, although sills can be cast in place. They must also be placed in a lower position in the wall than the smaller windows so that steel **reinforced** lintels can be poured in place above them. A lintel built of concrete blocks set on an angle-iron can also be used for larger windows.

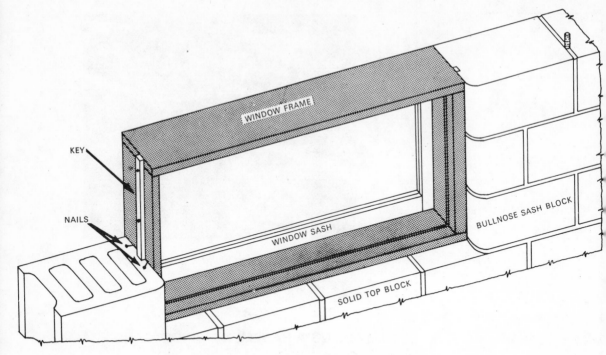

The nails will be locked in the mortar joint.

mesh: Cross woven wire screen or expanded sheet steel.

PARTITION WALLS OF CONCRETE BLOCK

Concrete block partition walls are built up at the same time as the outer walls. The walls are not bonded together by overlapping the blocks. Instead, they are tied together by strips of metal plaster lath or wire **mesh** placed in every other mortar joint of non-load bearing parti-

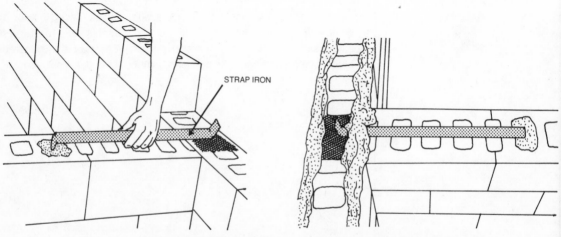

A method of tying partitions to the outside wall—nonload bearing.

tions, and by metal straps in every fourth joint of load bearing partitions. The drawings show both of these methods. The joint between the walls should be filled with mortar. It should then be raked out to a 19 mm depth and filled with **caulking compound**.

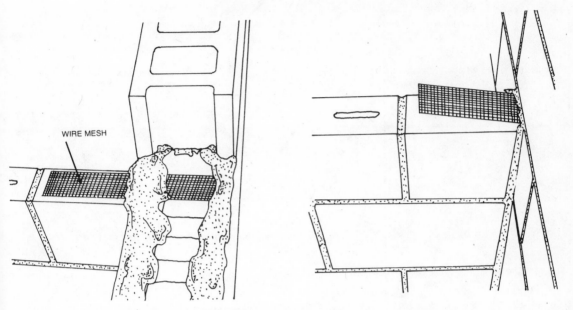

WIRE MESH

A method of tying partitions to the outside wall—load bearing.

caulking: A waterproof material used to seal joints in buildings. The rubber compound types do not harden and crack with age.

parging: A coat of cement plaster applied to poured concrete or block walls to help seal them and improve their appearance.

PARGING A CONCRETE BLOCK WALL

When the walls of the block foundation have been completed, they should be given two 6 mm coats of mortar. This process is called **parging**. The mortar used to lay the blocks is also used for the parging operation. It is spread on the wall from the footings to 150 mm above the ground level of the graded building lot. In some cases, the whole outside surface of the walls is parged.

For a thoroughly watertight basement, add a prepared sealer to the mortar. Use the amount indicated on the manufacturer's label. A hawk and plastering trowel are used to apply the mortar.

To parge a concrete wall:

1. Sprinkle the wall with water just before parging it to prevent the parging from drying out too rapidly.
2. Spread on the first mortar coat and before it hardens, roughen the surface with a wire scratcher. This will make the bond with the second coat tighter. Form a rounded cover of mortar at the joint between the wall and the footing. As the first coat hardens, very fine cracks will form. These will be covered by the second coat of parging.

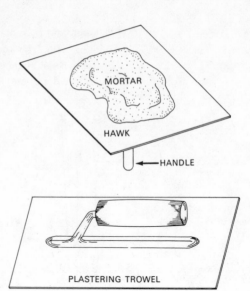

The tools needed for the parging operation.

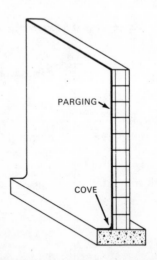

The cove improves the run-off of water to the weeping tile.

3. Apply the second coat after the first has been allowed to harden for at least twenty-four hours. Dampen the first coat. Then apply the mortar with a firm pressure on the trowel to bond the two layers together. The wall area above grade may be trowelled smooth or patterned with a regular, fanning motion of the trowel. A uniformly rough surface can be made by sponging the fresh mortar with a wet burlap bag.

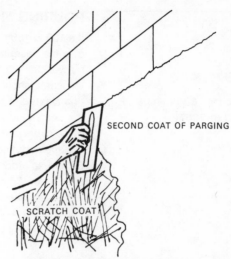

SECOND COAT OF PARGING

SCRATCH COAT

Applying the second coat of parging mortar.

4. Brush on two coats of tar, covering the wall from the footing cove to within 50 mm of ground level. This same operation should also be performed on poured concrete walls that are below grade.

   When the tar has had time to dry, the excavated area around the foundation wall may be filled. Build up a deep layer of gravel above the weeping tile, then complete the back filling with the earth that was previously removed from the excavation. If a bulldozer is used to push the earth into place, the machine must be kept well back on solid ground to prevent its weight from damaging the new wall.

TAR (2 COATS)

Two coats of tar over the parging make the wall more waterproof.

debris: Bits and pieces of building materials.

POURING THE BASEMENT FLOOR

If a 100 to 150 mm layer of gravel or crushed stone was spread evenly over the basement floor area when the footings were completed, it will be well-packed by the time the foundation walls have been built. Any low spots should be filled, and the whole area should be raked level and cleared of **debris**. If drain pipes or water pipes are to run under the floor, they should be installed at this time. If the soil is still wet, place overlapping sheets of polyethylene film over the gravel.

Basement floors in houses are poured to a minimum thickness of 89 mm. In order to make the floor level, or to provide a slope toward a floor drain, 38 mm by 89 mm screeds are set on edge, levelled and nailed to stakes. Place the screeds 2400 to 3000 mm apart.

Pipe having a 32 mm outside diameter and resting on Y-shaped supports is also used as screeding. The supports are left in the concrete.

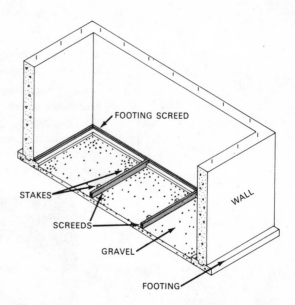

The screeds control the thickness and flatness of the floor.

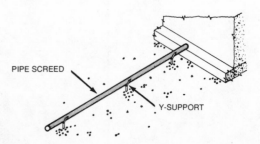

A pipe screed is easily removed and leaves a smaller area to be filled.

Footing screeds should be laid on top of the footing and next to the wall. Screeds around a floor drain are laid to slope down toward the drain.

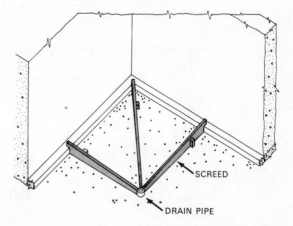

Screeds installed around a floor drain establish the floor slope.

To pour the footing forms:

1. Beginning at one corner of the basement, pour the area behind the first screed. Thoroughly spade it along the footings, and immediately screed it level with a straight-edge made of 38 mm by 140 mm lumber long enough to more than span the distance between the screeds. Keep a small amount of concrete along the straight-edge and fill in any slightly hollow areas.

2. When the area on both sides of a screed has been levelled with a straight-edge, that screed is then lifted out and the space is filled with concrete.

3. The final smooth surface finish is achieved by using a float and then a trowel. The concrete should be hard enough to support the weight of the worker, yet be in workable condition. The floating operation pushes the coarse aggregate slightly below the surface and the trowel is then able to make a smoother finish.

CHAPTER 5

House Framing
Styles and
Materials

HOUSE FRAMING STYLES

WATCH FOR THESE WORDS

subfloor   joists
studs   rafters
plates

HOW TO USE THESE WORDS

1. The **subfloor** is usually made of plywood.
2. A wall frame is made up of **studs** and **plates**.
3. Only straight lengths of lumber should be used as **joists**.
4. **Rafters** are part of the roof frame.

FIND THE ANSWERS TO THESE QUESTIONS

1. State three reasons why wood framing is used by most house builders.
2. Describe the location and use of the following frame pieces:
   (a) sill
   (b) joist

(c) stud

(d) plate

(e) rafter

3. Name four styles of wood framing.

4. What framing method was used to construct the house you live in?

5. If you were building a house for yourself, which framing method would you use? Why?

6. Name four kinds of trees used to make framing lumber.

7. What do the annual rings on a log represent?

8. List the standard widths of rough sawed lumber.

9. Describe two methods of drying lumber.

10. List the standard thicknesses of rough lumber.

11. What are the standard lengths of building lumber?

12. List the standard sizes of S4S framing lumber.

13. What does S4S mean?

14. List three common defects found in framing lumber.

Wood framing is used in nine out of ten houses in Canada. The building may be covered with stucco or brick veneer but its frame is constructed in the same way as a house with wood lap siding.

There are several reasons for the popularity of wood as a framing material. Wood is much less expensive than steel, it provides much better insulation than solid masonry construction, and it is the easiest type of construction material to work with. Buildings of any shape and design are possible with wood.

The long lifespan of well-built wood framing is shown by the fact that some of the oldest buildings in Canada are of this type.

Not all wood frames are alike. In fact, there are four popular styles of wood frames used in house construction today: platform frame, balloon frame, braced frame, and the modern post-and-beam frame.

PLATFORM FRAME

The platform frame is by far the most commonly used framing style, especially for single-storey houses. The floor framing and the **subfloor** extend to the outer edges of the building and provide a platform on which to build and fasten the wall framing.

This frame is considered the easiest to build because the wall **studs** are short, and because it is often possible to build whole walls or sections flat on the floor or in a factory. The sections are then lifted into position and nailed to the platform.

subfloor: A wooden floor nailed onto the floor framing. The finish flooring is laid on the subfloor.

studs: The vertical pieces in a wall frame.

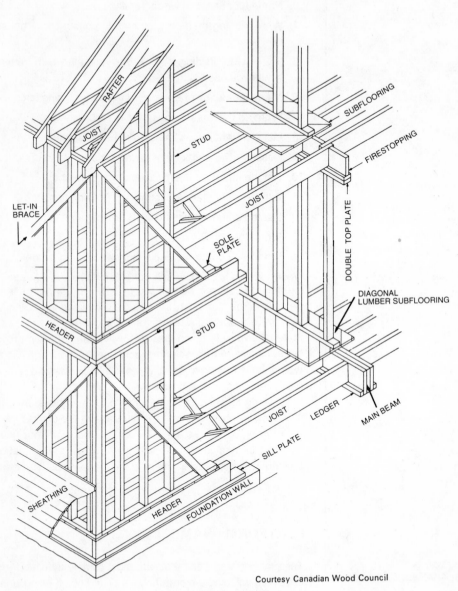

Courtesy Canadian Wood Council

A platform house frame.

A worker nailing together the frame of a wall.

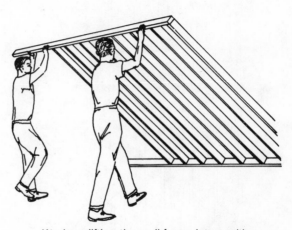

Workers lifting the wall frame into position.

BALLOON FRAME

plates: The horizontal pieces in a wall frame. Also the sill plate, which is bolted to the foundation.

The balloon frame is popular for two-storey house construction. Exterior wall studs rest directly on the **sill plate** and rise the full two storeys to the top **plate**. The second floor joists rest on a 19 mm by 89 mm strip let into the wall studs at the correct height.

Where interior walls on both floors are located one above the other, they are framed as shown in the drawing. This makes the entire frame more resistant to twisting and settling out of shape when the parts of the frame shrink or expand. Notice that wood blocking is used between the studs at the second floor level as firestops. A fire in any wall section will not spread as easily to other sections when firestops are used.

Combination platform and balloon frames are also used as shown here. The outside walls rest on the first floor platform.

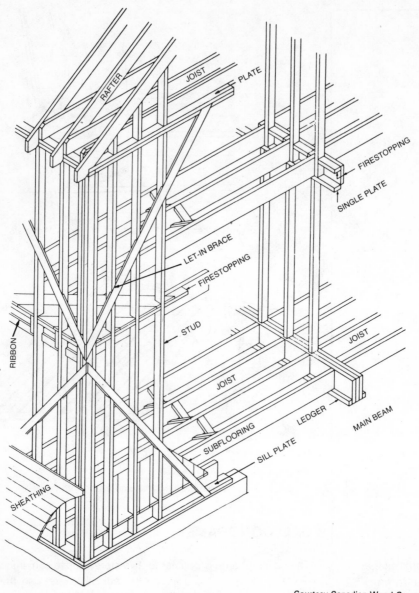

RAFTER
JOIST
PLATE
FIRESTOPPING
SINGLE PLATE
LET-IN BRACE
FIRESTOPPING
STUD
RIBBON
JOIST
JOIST
LEDGER
MAIN BEAM
SUBFLOORING
SILL PLATE
SHEATHING

Courtesy Canadian Wood Council

Balloon frame construction.

BRACED FRAME

Braced framing is probably the oldest style of frame construction. The framework was originally made of heavy timber. Modern sizes of lumber have caused a gradual change from the original style to the one shown opposite.

The built-up corner post in the drawing extends all the way from the sill to the top plate. These posts are also placed 3 to 4.5 m apart along the exterior walls. These built-up posts replace the solid, heavy timber posts that were used in older buildings. The sill and plates at the second floor and roof level, once framed with heavy timbers, are now built as shown in the drawing. Notice the extensive use of fire-stop blocks.

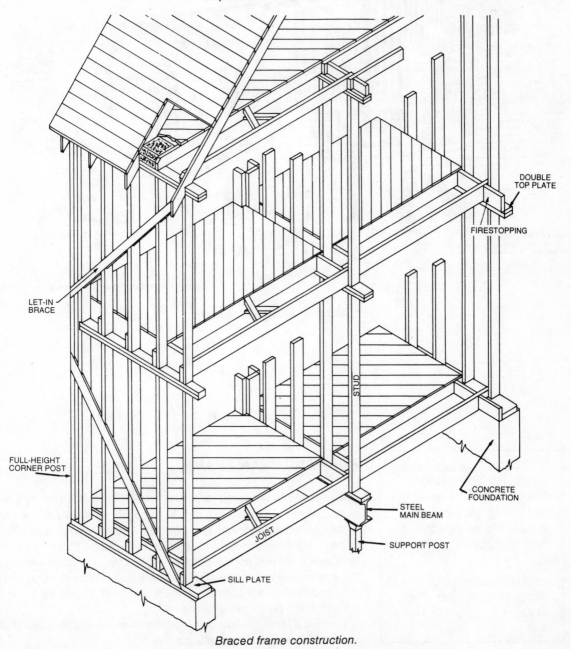

DOUBLE TOP PLATE

FIRESTOPPING

LET-IN BRACE

STUD

FULL-HEIGHT CORNER POST

CONCRETE FOUNDATION

STEEL MAIN BEAM

SUPPORT POST

JOIST

SILL PLATE

Braced frame construction.

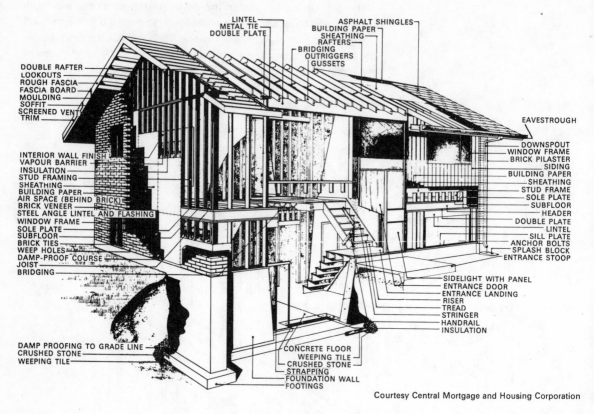

The parts of a modern frame house.

Courtesy Central Mortgage and Housing Corporation

joists: Horizontal pieces placed on edge in floor and ceiling frames. Joists are used to support the flooring materials.

rafters: The framing pieces that form the shape of a roof.

POST-AND-BEAM FRAME

The post-and-beam frame is a modern framing method for single-storey houses. The walls are built in much the same way as for the braced frame, but the floor and roof have beams spaced from 1200 to 2400 mm on centre instead of **joists** and **rafters**. Planking which is 38 mm or 64 mm thick is used for subflooring and roof sheathing. The beams and the underside of the planking are often finished with stain and varnish to reduce the amount of material used on the interior and to add height to the ceilings.

There is a definite saving in materials with this method but the greatest saving is in time and labour.

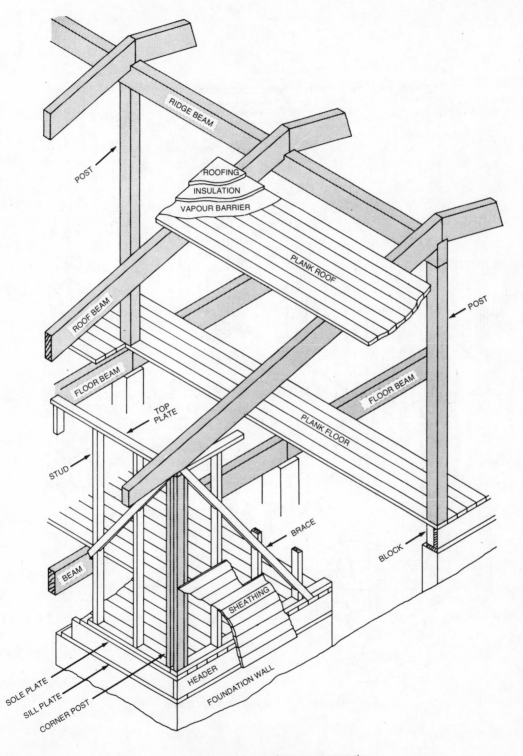

RIDGE BEAM

POST

ROOFING

INSULATION

VAPOUR BARRIER

ROOF BEAM

PLANK ROOF

POST

FLOOR BEAM

FLOOR BEAM

TOP PLATE

PLANK FLOOR

STUD

BRACE

BLOCK

BEAM

SHEATHING

SOLE PLATE

SILL PLATE

CORNER POST

HEADER

FOUNDATION WALL

Post-and-beam frame construction.

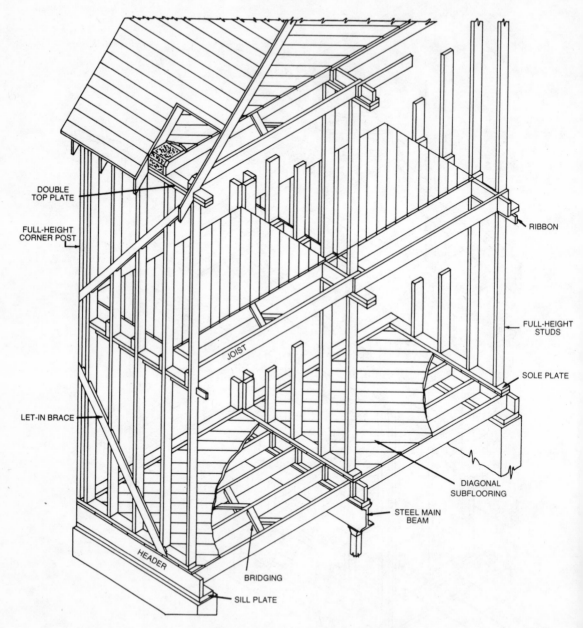

DOUBLE
TOP PLATE

FULL-HEIGHT
CORNER POST

RIBBON

FULL-HEIGHT
STUDS

JOIST

SOLE PLATE

LET-IN BRACE

DIAGONAL
SUBFLOORING

STEEL MAIN
BEAM

HEADER

BRIDGING

SILL PLATE

A combination balloon and platform frame.

BUILDING MATERIALS

WATCH FOR THESE WORDS

grain	warp
kiln	veneer

HOW TO USE THESE WORDS

1. **Grain** and colour make wood attractive.
2. Lumber may be dried quickly in a **kiln**.
3. Wood will often **warp** as it dries.
4. Plywood is made of thin sheets of **veneer**.

FIND THE ANSWERS TO THESE QUESTIONS

1. Find the volume of each of the following lumber orders:
   (a) One hundred pieces of fir, 38 mm thick, 89 mm wide, and 3.66 m long.
   (b) 2000 pieces of spruce, 38 mm thick, 286 mm wide, and 4.88 m long.
   (c) Thirty pieces of pine, 19 mm thick, 140 mm wide, and 3.05 m long.
2. Find the total cost of each of the following lumber orders:
   (a) Ten pieces of spruce, 38 mm by 89 mm by 2.44 m, priced at $1.00 per metre.
   (b) Fifty pieces of 38 mm by 184 mm cedar, 3.66 m long, priced at $3.00 per metre.
   (c) 1000 pieces of 19 mm pine trim, 4.88 m long, priced at $1.20 per metre.
3. How much will a builder have to pay for 250 pieces of 38 mm by 184 mm spruce in lengths of 3.05 m, when the price is $350.00 per cubic metre?

FRAMING LUMBER

When the great logs of pine, spruce, fir and cedar are hauled out of the bush country and hoisted onto huge trucks or rail cars, they are on their way to the sawmill to be sawed into lumber.

First the bark is removed and the log is squared. The planks or boards made by these squaring cuts have bark along their edges. This bark is sawed off later.

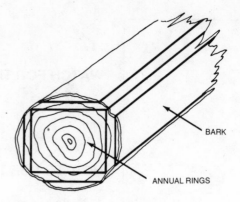

Squaring a log. The outer bark slabs cannot be used for lumber.

The remainder of the log is then sawed into standard thicknesses of 25 mm, 51 mm, 76 mm, or 102 mm lumber.

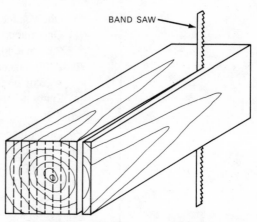

Sawing a squared log to make lumber.

grain: The pattern of lines in wood. It is caused by the difference in size between spring and summer growth cells.

The pattern of **grain** lines in each piece of lumber is caused by the yearly growth of the tree. When you look at the end of a log, these growth lines show up in the form of rough circles called annual rings. The distance between any pair of annual rings shows the amount of growth of the tree during one year.

The wide slabs of lumber cut from squared logs are then cut into standard widths and lengths of framing lumber. Standard rough cut lumber is found in the following widths:

51 mm	203 mm
102 mm	254 mm
152 mm	305 mm

and in the following lengths:

2.40 m	5.49 m
3.05 m	6.10 m
3.66 m	6.71 m
4.27 m	7.32 m
4.88 m	

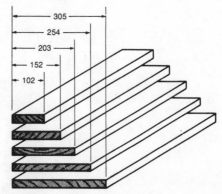

Standard widths of rough lumber, in millimetres.

DRYING LUMBER

Lumber that has just been sawed from the log is still green; that is, it still contains a great deal of tree sap which must be removed before the lumber can be used for building construction.

One method of drying lumber is to stack it outdoors in piles with cross straps between the layers so that air can circulate between the boards to evaporate the sap.

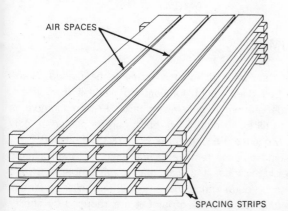

Courtesy Department of Lands and Forests

Rough lumber stacked for air drying.

kiln: A building for drying large amounts of lumber. The speed and amount of drying can be carefully controlled.

A much better and faster way to dry lumber is to dry it in a **kiln**. The lumber is piled in the same way as for air drying in a closed room or building. Hot, dry air is circulated through and around the pile of lumber for several hours.

With either method, the moisture in the wood evaporates into the air. By controlling the amount of heat and the length of time the wood remains in the kiln, the correct degree of dryness can be carefully obtained. The best grades of framing lumber are kiln dried. As a piece of lumber dries, it shrinks slightly.

Courtesy Moore Dry Kiln Company of Canada Ltd.,
Brampton, Ont.

A kiln for controlled drying of rough lumber.

PLANING LUMBER

After the lumber has been dried, it is ready to be planed. Some lumber dealers buy dried, rough lumber and plane it themselves, while others order it from large planing mills. Framing lumber is usually planed on all four sides (S4S), but it can be planed on only one side (S1S), two sides (S2S), or three sides (S3S) if desired.

Since the planing process removes a thin layer of wood, planed lumber is smaller in thickness and width than rough lumber. A 51 mm by 102 mm piece of rough lumber becomes 38 mm thick by 89 mm wide (SI standards). Other sizes of lumber are reduced by similar amounts.

When talking about or ordering construction lumber, always state its planed size. All construction lumber is kiln dried and **S4S**, so that the modern carpenter only needs to know the standard planed sizes. For framing lumber these are:

38 mm by 89 mm
38 mm by 140 mm
38 mm by 184 mm
38 mm by 235 mm
38 mm by 286 mm

A thickness planer in operation.

LUMBER DEFECTS

warp: Any change in lumber from a straight, flat surface. Warp is caused by uneven shrinkage while drying.

Warp in lumber is shown in the drawings. As wood dries, it shrinks on all sides. The side closest to the bark of the tree always shrinks more than the other side, and the board warps. If the lumber has been dried properly, the warp will be slight and will be removed during planing.

Checks are sometimes called splits and are breaks along the grain lines, usually at the end of the board. They are commonly seen in air dried lumber where the hot sun has caused the ends to dry too fast.

Knots in a piece of wood show where a limb or branch has grown out from the tree trunk. When the knots are large and loose, the lumber will be very weak, but small, tight knots should not affect its strength. A few knots in a long piece of lumber usually give it an ugly appearance, but in recent years, knotty pine has become popular as an inside wall covering.

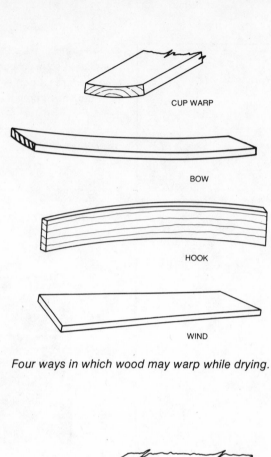

CUP WARP

BOW

HOOK

WIND

Four ways in which wood may warp while drying.

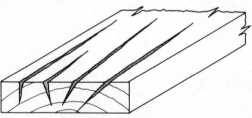

The appearance of end check.

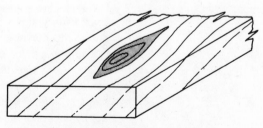

The appearance of a knot.

MEASURING IN THE METRIC SYSTEM

Softwood lumber is measured and sold by the lineal metre and the cubic metre.

Lineal Measure:

To find the number of lineal metres in any piece of wood, measure its length. The cost is found by multiplying the number of lineal metres in the length by the price per lineal metre.

Example:

A 38 mm by 89 mm piece of spruce, 3.66 m long, and priced at $1.00 per lineal metre, would cost:

$3.66 \times \$1.00 = \$3.66$

An order of 20 of these spruce pieces would cost:

$\$3.66 \times 20 = \$73.20$

Cubic Measure:

The cubic measurement of lumber involves finding its volume.

$$\text{Volume} = \frac{T \times W}{1\ 000\ 000} \times L = m^3$$

where T = thickness: mm

W = width: mm

L = length: m

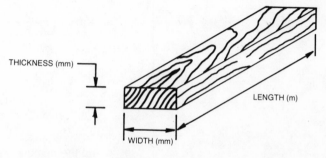

Measuring lumber.

Example:

Find the metric volume of a 38 mm by 140 mm piece of fir, 3.05 m long.

$$\text{Volume} = \frac{38 \times 140}{1\ 000\ 000} \times 3.05 = 0.038 \times 0.140 \times 3.05 = 0.016\ m^3$$

If the price of fir is \$400.00 per cubic metre, this piece would cost:

$0.016 \times \$400.00 = \$6.40$

MEASURING LUMBER IN THE IMPERIAL SYSTEM

Lumber is measured and sold by either the lineal foot or the board foot. To find the number of lineal feet in any piece of lumber you have to measure only its length. Its cost is found by multiplying the number of lineal feet by the price per lineal foot.

Example:

A 2 in. by 4 in. piece of spruce, 10 ft. long, and priced at 12¢ (\$.12) per lineal foot would cost:

$10 \times \$.12 = \$1.20$

One board foot of lumber is 12 in. wide, 12 in. long, and 1 in. thick.

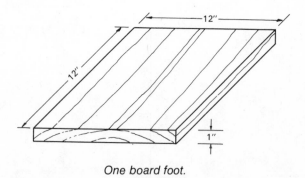

One board foot.

If all lumber were 12 in. wide and 1 in. thick, it would be a simple matter to find the number of board feet in each piece by measuring its length as with lineal measure. However, since this is not the case, it is necessary to use arithmetic again. The number of board feet in any piece of lumber can be found by using the following formula:

$$\frac{T \times W}{12} \times L$$

where T = thickness: in.

W = width: in.

L = length: ft.

Example:

Find the board measure of a piece of lumber 2 in.thick, 4 in.wide, and 12 ft.long.

$$\frac{2 \times 4}{12} \times 12 = \frac{8}{12} \times 12 = 8 \text{ board ft.}$$

The cost of this 2 by 4 lumber can be found by multiplying the 8 board ft.by the price per board foot.

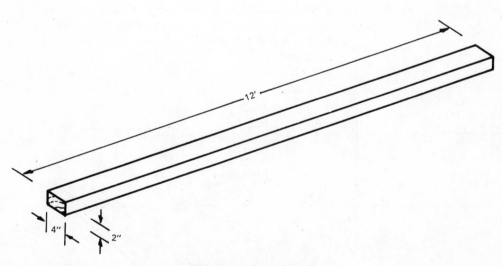

Eight board feet of lumber.

SHEATHING MATERIALS

FIND THE ANSWERS TO THESE QUESTIONS

1. How does plywood cut down on the time and work involved in building?
2. How should plywood sheets be stored?
3. What is the correct name for the thin layers of wood used to make a sheet of plywood?
4. What is the standard width of plywood sheets?
5. What is the standard length of plywood sheets?
6. What is the standard size of fiberboard sheets?
7. Why is fiberboard so popular as a sheathing material for outside walls?
8. What materials are used to make the newest type of wall sheathing?
9. Why is this new sheathing likely to become popular?

PLYWOOD

The use of plywood in the building industry has cut down on much of the time and work involved in covering the framework and has resulted in far stronger buildings. With plywood sheathing, the building is braced in all directions, and extra frame bracing is not needed.

Plywood is made from thin sheets of wood glued together with water resistant glue so that the grain in each sheet runs crosswise to the ones next to it. This helps prevent the sheets from warping. Even so, plywood should always be stored flat on the floor to make sure that it stays flat.

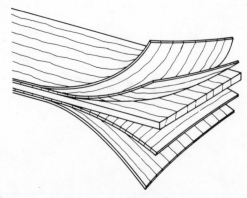

Illustrating the direction of grain in each ply of a sheet of plywood.

veneer: Thin sheets of wood used to make plywood.

The thin layers of wood are called **veneer**. This veneer is made by revolving straight logs in a large veneer cutting lathe. A very sharp, stiff blade slices a continuous layer of wood off the log as it turns.

The standard size of plywood sheets used in building construction is 1200 mm wide by 2400 mm long. Sheets 1220 mm by 2440 mm are also manufactured. Thicknesses of plywood sheathing are:

7.5 mm	15.5 mm
9.5 mm	18.5 mm
12.5 mm	

Sheathing-grade plywood is not finish sanded and may have a few knots in the veneer. The better grades have one or both sides clear of flaws and are smooth sanded. Top grades are often prefinished for use as interior wall covering. Edges are left squared, or are machined for tongue-and-groove or lap matching. Standard thicknesses of sanded plywood sheets are:

6 mm	14 mm
8 mm	17 mm
11 mm	19 mm

Small orders of plywood are priced and sold by the sheet. Large quantites are priced and sold in units of 100 m^2. The price will vary according to the thickness, grade and kind of wood used as finish veneer.

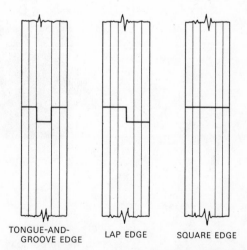

TONGUE-AND-
GROOVE EDGE   LAP EDGE   SQUARE EDGE

Plywood sheets are edge matched in these three styles.

FIBERBOARD

Fiberboard is a manufactured sheet material; it is soft, has a light mass and is finished in several ways for a variety of uses. At present asphalt treated fiberboard is the most popular sheathing material for exterior walls because it is inexpensive, strong, and water and wind resistant. The photograph shows a house frame covered with this type of fiberboard.

Fiberboard being used for exterior wall sheathing.

Some manufacturers shape the edges of fiberboard sheets for a more windproof joint. Untreated fiberboard is often used as an interior wall covering in cottages, attic rooms and closets, where it also serves as insulation.

Standard sheets are 12 mm thick, 1200 mm wide, and 2400 mm long.

Shaped edges of fiberboard sheets.

The newest type of sheathing material is made of fiberglass with aluminum foil on both sides of the sheet. Both fiberglass and aluminum are good heat insulators. Walls framed with 38 mm by 89 mm lumber, and sheathed with the fiberglass and aluminum sheets, provide about the same amount of heat insulation as walls framed with 38 mm by 140 mm lumber and covered with fiberboard or plywood. With fuel costs rising, you can expect to see more of this new product being used. It is known on the market by various trade names. You may buy it by asking for fiberglass/aluminum foil products.

CHAPTER 6

Platform
Floo
Framing

BUILDING SILLS

WATCH FOR THESE WORDS

sill	spirit
preservative	header
mortar	

HOW TO USE THESE WORDS

1. The **header** and **sill** are fastened together like an "L" or an upside down "T" ($\perp$).
2. Some framing lumber is treated with a **preservative** before it i used.
3. Hollows in the top of a foundation may be filled with **mortar**.
4. A **spirit** level is used to see whether a surface is truly horizontal c vertical.

FIND THE ANSWERS TO THESE QUESTIONS

1. Why must the sill plate be bolted very securely to the foundation?
2. What sizes of lumber are used for sill plates?

3. How may sills be damaged when the foundation wall is less than 300 mm above ground?

4. How far back from the face of the foundation wall should the sill plate be positioned?

5. Why should the position of each anchor bolt be measured separately?

6. Why are oversized mounting holes drilled?

7. When must the sill plate be set in a bed of wet mortar?

8. Describe the location of the header for a box sill and for a T-sill.

The **sill** plate is the building anchor. It is bolted solidly to the foundation to prevent gradual shifting of the framework.

sill: A flat, horizontal piece of lumber bolted to the foundation to hold and support the frame of a building.

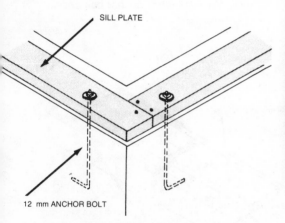

SILL PLATE

12 mm ANCHOR BOLT

Sill plates bolted to foundation wall.

Straight lengths of 38 mm lumber, 89 mm, 140 mm, or 184 mm wide, are held in place by 12 mm bolts spaced 1200 to 1800 mm apart. The bolts must be placed in position during the construction of the foundation wall. Short pieces of the sill plate should be held by at least two bolts.

If the top of the foundation wall is less than 300 mm above ground level, the sill should be coated with a chemical wood **preservative** to prevent wood rot caused by ground dampness. Metal flashing or plastic damp proofing may be placed under the sill.

preservative: A liquid material that protects wood against water damage.

To install a sill plate:

1. Select a straight length of lumber and place it on the foundation wall against the anchor bolts as shown.

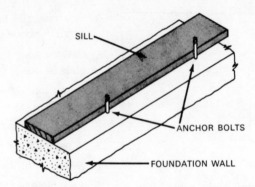

Position sill plate against anchor bolts.

2. Hold a steel framing square against the edge of the sill so that the tongue of the square is against an anchor bolt and mark along the tongue with a pencil. Mark the other anchor bolt positions in the same way.

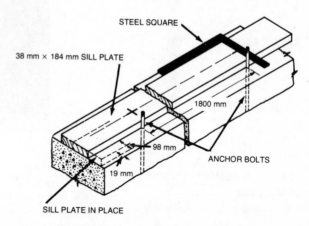

Squaring a line across the sill plate at each bolt.

3. Find the distance from the outer edge of the foundation wall to the centre of each anchor bolt.

4. Take this measurement and subtract the thickness of the rough wall sheathing. Mark the sill plate at each bolt location line, as shown.

Since the anchor bolts have been set in wet **mortar** or concrete, they may have shifted slightly and will not all be the same distance from the edge of the wall. Measure each one separately. The illustration shows a 19 mm allowance for sheathing.

mortar: A mixture of cement, lime, sand and water that hardens through hydration.

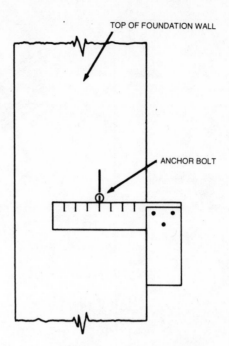

Measure each bolt location.

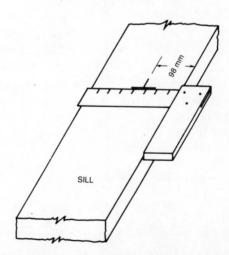

Mark bolt location on sill plate. Allow for thickness of sheathing and in some cases brick veneer thickness.

5. Bore a 19 mm hole at each of the bolt locations and place the sill plate in position on the wall. The oversized holes allow you to shift the sill slightly to make it perfectly straight.

6. Mark the ends of the sill with a square and saw them off with a cross-cut saw.

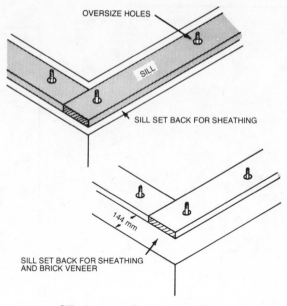

Sill plates positioned on wall.

OVERSIZE HOLES

SILL

SILL SET BACK FOR SHEATHING

144 mm

SILL SET BACK FOR SHEATHING
AND BRICK VENEER

spirit: A type of alcohol, usually methyl hydrate. The air bubble trapped in this alcohol is used to show if something is level.

7. With the sill plate in position, place large, flat washers over the bolts, start the nuts and turn them down to pull the sill tight against the foundation wall.

8. Check all along the sill plate with a **spirit** level. If the plate is not level, it will have to be removed and set in a layer of wet mortar for levelling. When the foundation wall is level, caulk the joint between the wall and the sill plate to seal any small openings.

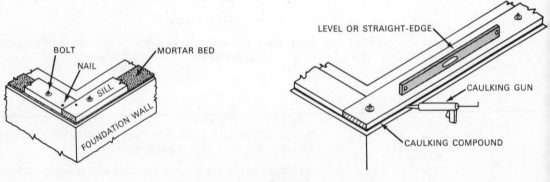

BOLT
NAIL
MORTAR BED
SILL
FOUNDATION WALL

LEVEL OR STRAIGHT-EDGE
CAULKING GUN
CAULKING COMPOUND

Levelling and caulking the sill plates.

9. If the building plans call for a double sill plate, the upper plate should lap over the joint in the lower plate at the corners. The anchor bolts should pass through both plates. The plates should be nailed together every 600 mm with two 75 mm nails.

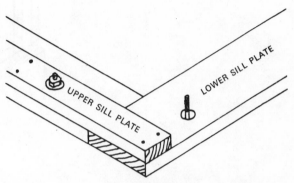

Double sill plate lapped at corners.

header: The outer part of a floor frame. It is made of floor joist materials and closes off the ends of the joists.

10. Place the **header** in position on the sill plate and toenail it to the plate with 75 mm nails, 300 to 450 mm apart. Nail the headers together at the corners.

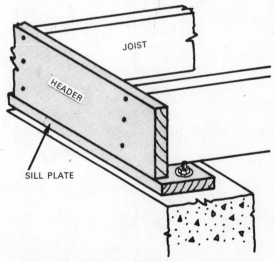

Box or L-type of sill header nailed in position.

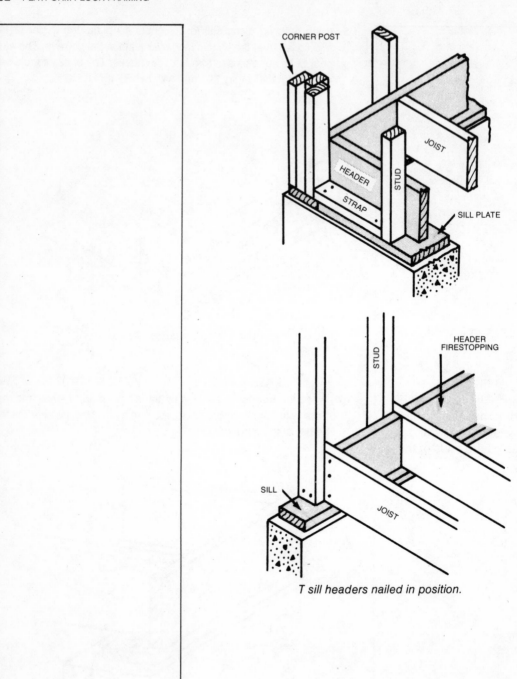

T sill headers nailed in position.

MAIN BEAMS

WATCH FOR THESE WORDS

laminated   pedestal
dowel

HOW TO USE THESE WORDS

1. **Laminated** beams are often used to support the roofs of large modern buildings.
2. A steel **dowel** may be used to fasten a wood post to a concrete **pedestal**.

FIND THE ANSWERS TO THESE QUESTIONS

1. Name four styles of wood main beam.
2. Describe two ways of positioning the ends of the main beam.
3. What is the purpose of a wood or metal cap on the support posts?
4. What equipment will be needed to level the main beam?
5. What method is used to keep the support post from slipping off its footing?

The main beam is a heavy length of steel or wood. In most houses, it stretches from one end foundation wall to the other and supports about one-quarter of the building's weight. When an architect designs a house, he very carefully calculates the size of the main beam and the number and location of the support posts it will need. The carpenter should follow the blueprints exactly.

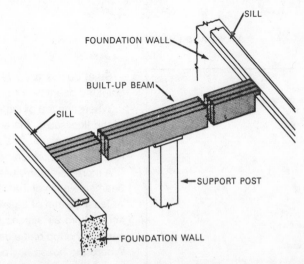

Built-up main beam in position on walls and support post.

> **laminated:** Made up of many layers fastened firmly together, usually with glue.

The illustrations show the common types of main beams used in house construction. Note that the joints in built-up wood beams are made directly over the support posts.

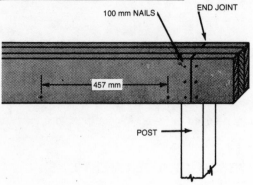

A built-in wood beam. Notice nail spacing.

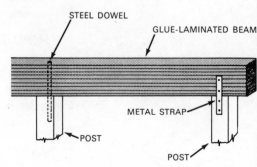

A glue-laminated wood beam.

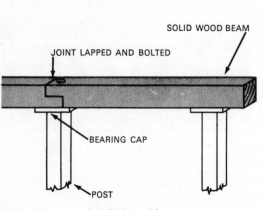

A solid wood beam.

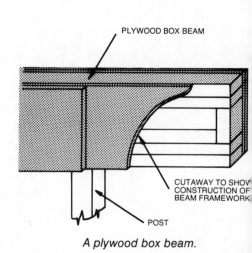

A plywood box beam.

Steel beams are available in many sizes and shapes. Be sure to paint the beam with a rust preventing paint before installing it.

Where the top of the main beam is to be installed level with the top of the floor joists, the ends of the beam rest on the sill plate and are toenailed in place. This method provides the greatest amount of headroom in the basement.

A more commonly used method is to rest the floor joists on the main beam; the ends of the beam are set into pockets in the foundation wall. At least 92 mm of beam should rest flat on the bottom of the pocket, and 12 mm air spaces should be provided at the end and sides. Of course, the top of the beam must be level with the top of the sill plate. Where the house has no basement, the underside of the main beam must be at least 460 mm above ground level.

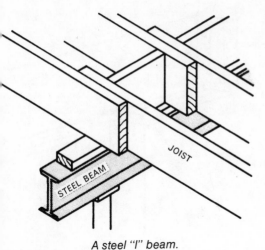

A steel "I" beam.

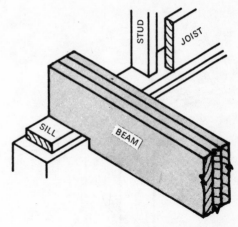

Main beam resting on the sill plate.

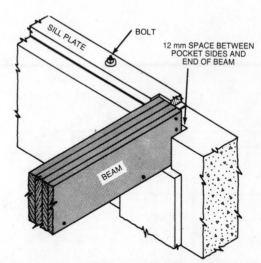

Main beam set in a pocket in the foundation wall.

dowel: A round pin used to fasten two pieces of material together.

The location and size of the beam supporting posts are just as carefully calculated as the size of the main beam itself, and again the carpenter must follow the blueprints. The posts may be of solid wood, built-up wood, steel, concrete block or poured concrete construction.

Solid or built-up wooden posts should be fitted with a wood or metal cap for fastening to the main beam. They can also be held in place by a steel **dowel** or metal straps.

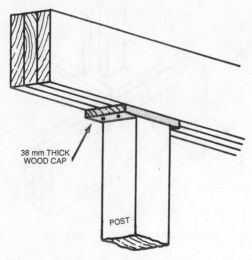

A wooden bearing cap for a main-beam post.

38 mm THICK WOOD CAP

POST

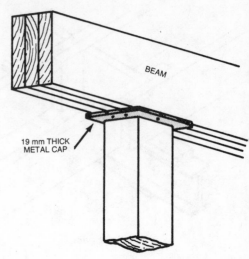

A metal bearing cap for a main-beam post.

BEAM

19 mm THICK METAL CAP

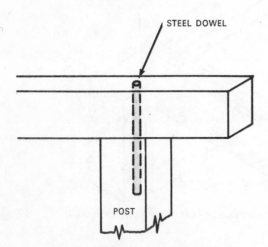

Beam and post held by steel dowel.

STEEL DOWEL

POST

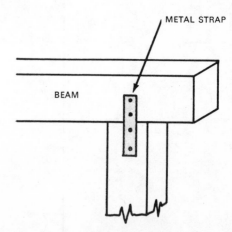

Beam held in place by a steel strap on both sides.

METAL STRAP

BEAM

The base of the post should rest on a masonry footing and be held in place by a metal dowel embedded (partially sunk) in the footing. The footing extends at least 50 mm above the basement floor or 150 mm above the ground if there is no basement.

pedestal: A raised base or platform.

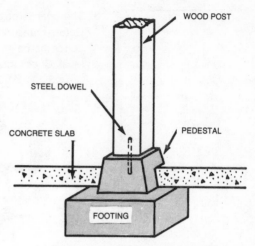

Support footing for wood posts.

To install the main beam:

1. Cut the beam square at both ends so that a 12 mm air space will be left in each wall pocket.

2. Lift the beam into position. If the top of the beam is lower than the sill plate, place a steel bearing block of the correct thickness under each end.

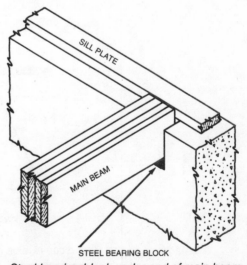

Steel bearing block under end of main beam.

3. The beam would tend to sag if it were supported only at its ends. Before measuring and cutting the support posts, place screw jacks under the beam near the post locations and lift the beam until it is level. Check the whole length of the beam with a spirit level.

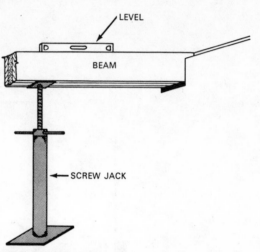

Levelling the beam with a screw jack and level.

4. Square one end of each post and raise it into position on its footing with the upper end against the beam. Mark the post along the beam for cutting. The base of the post should be positioned toward one side of the footing to keep the post vertical.

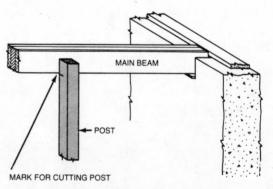

Marking the posts for cutting to length.

5. If a cap is to be used on the post, allow for its thickness and cut the post off square.

6. Bore a hole in the base of the post to fit over the metal pin and fasten the cap to the top of the post.

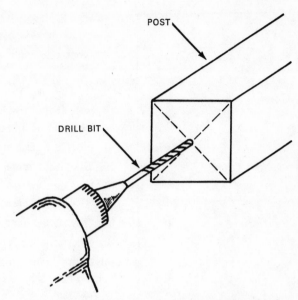

Mark the post from corner to corner to locate dowel hole.

7. Raise the main beam out of position. This allows you to slide the posts over their locating pins. Then lower the main beam into position on the posts. Check to see that the beam is still level.

8. Fasten the top of the posts to the main beam.

FRAMING FOR THE FLOOR

WATCH FOR THESE WORDS

crown   **ledger**
toenail

HOW TO USE THESE WORDS

1. The **crowned** edges of floor joists should be turned upwards to prevent the floor from sagging.
2. Sometimes the floor joists rest on a **ledger** and are **toenailed** to the main beam.

FIND THE ANSWERS TO THESE QUESTIONS

1. Why is it so important to use joist material of the correct size for floor framing?
2. What is the largest recommended joist length?
3. Why should the joist locations be marked on the header as well as the sill plate?

4. Why is it important to always start at the same end of the building to mark out the main beam and both sill plates?

5. What size nails should be used to fasten the header to the joists?

6. Why should the crowned edge of the joists be turned up?

7. How should the floor framing be constructed to support a load bearing wall that runs in the same direction as the joists?

8. What is a tail joist?

9. What is a trimmer joist?

10. How can the tail joists be supported until the opening headers are nailed in place?

11. Why should trimmer joists and headers be doubled?

12. When is it necessary to use joist hangers to frame an opening?

Joists are planks that are set on edge and stretched across the building from sill plate to sill plate. They are supported in the middle by the main beam. Because continuous joists of the proper length are expensive and difficult to obtain, two planks are usually butted and joined at the main beam to form the joist. At least 38 mm of the joists must be supported at each end. Remember that much of the weight of the building will be on the floor joists.

The size of the joists depends on their spacing and on the distance from the main beam to the sill plate. This distance is called the **joist span**. A load of 1.9 kN per 1 m^2 of floor area is used as a standard for the weight that the floor joists will have to support. The table below indicates the sizes of spruce joists needed to support 1.9 kN per 1 m^2 over a variety of spans. Joist spacing of 300 mm, 400 mm, or 600 mm is standard. This allows the use of standard sizes of plywood sheets for subflooring without having to cut every sheet.

SIZE	300 mm Spacing	400 mm Spacing	600 mm Spacing
38 mm by 140 mm	3.00 m	2.65 m	2.16 m
38 mm by 184 mm	3.96 m	3.49 m	2.85 m
38 mm by 235 mm	5.05 m	4.46 m	3.64 m
38 mm by 286 mm	6.15 m	5.42 m	4.43 m

Spruce joist spans.

Spans of more than 4.88 m are generally considered too long. Therefore, buildings wider than 9.76 m should have two main beams instead of just one. The complete framing of a floor with box sills is illustrated.

Courtesy Canadian Wood Council

A completed floor frame.

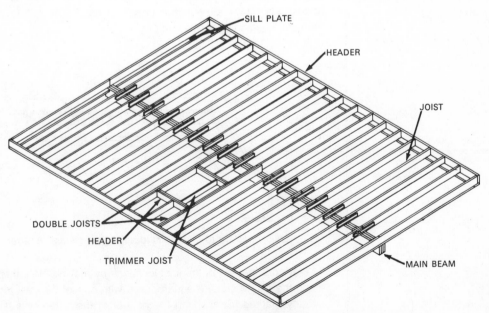

SILL PLATE

HEADER

JOIST

DOUBLE JOISTS

HEADER

TRIMMER JOIST

MAIN BEAM

The floor framing members.

To frame a floor with box sills:

1. Select a straight piece of wood strip, 2.44 m or 3.05 m long. Square one end, and using a steel tape measure, pencil mark the strip every 300 mm or 400 mm depending on the joist spacing to be used. Square a line across the strip at each mark and place an "X" beside each line on the side toward the squared end.

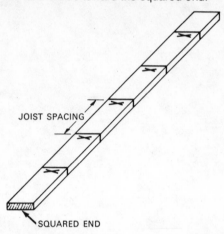

Making a pattern for marking joist locations.

2. Place this pattern strip on edge on the sill plate along one side wall so that its squared end rests against the header on the end wall. Mark the sill plate and header at each joist position, as shown in the illustration. The first joist should be marked 19 mm closer to the end header when plywood subflooring will be used. The pattern strip is then used beginning at this mark.

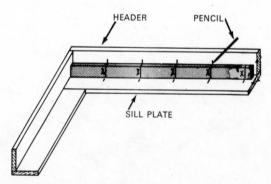

Using pattern to mark joist locations on sill and header.

3. Mark out the rest of the joist locations by moving the pattern strip along the sill. Match the squared end with one of the joist locations already marked. By marking the header at the same time, you are making sure the joists will be positioned vertically.

4. Mark the sill on the opposite wall and the main beam in the same way, **starting from the same end of the building**. If the joists are to be lapped at the main beam, the distance from the header to the first joist will be one joist thickness (38 mm) less than the spacing on the first wall. Otherwise the joists on this side of the building will be positioned on a slight angle.

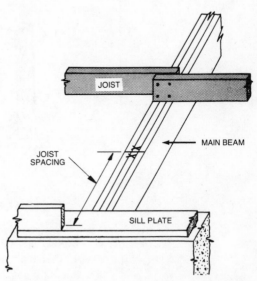

Marking location of lapped joists on main beam.

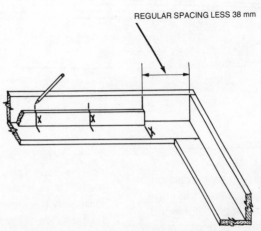

Locating the position of the first joist on the opposite wall.

5. Choose a particularly straight piece of joist material. Mark and square one end, measure the joist length and square the other end. If the end of the joists must fit over a double sill plate, measure, mark and cut it to fit.

crown: A high part on a surface.

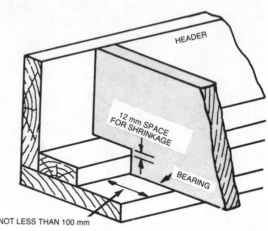

HEADER

12 mm SPACE FOR SHRINKAGE

BEARING

NOT LESS THAN 100 mm

A joist cut to fit over a double sill plate.

6. Use this first joist as a pattern to mark and cut all of the other joists. (Mark the first joist carefully so that you can recognize it among the others.) If some of the joist material is slightly bowed, be sure the **crowned** edge is the **top** of the joist.

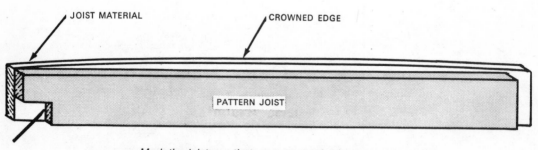

JOIST MATERIAL CROWNED EDGE

PATTERN JOIST

Mark the joists so that any crowned edges are up.

toenail: To drive nails on an angle, joining the edge or end of a piece of wood to the face of another piece.

7. Place the joists in position, one at a time, with the crowned edge up. Line them up with the lines marked on the sill and header so that the "X" mark is covered. Nail through the header into the ends of the joists with 100 mm nails. **Toenail** the joist to the sill with a 64 mm nail on each side of the joist.

8. Nail the joists in position on the main beam as shown in the illustrations.

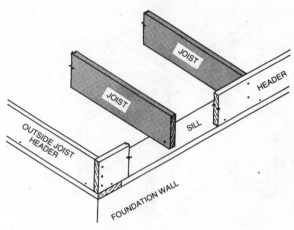

Joists positioned and nailed to the sill and header.

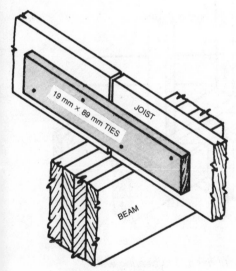

Butted and tied joists.

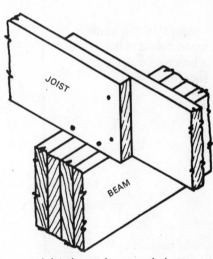

Joists lapped over main beam.

9. If the building will have a load bearing wall running in the same direction as the floor joists, a double joist should be installed at this location. A **load bearing wall** is a wall that supports part of the building above it.

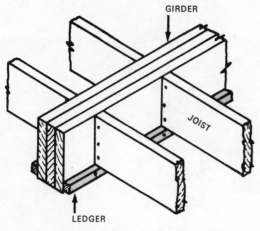

Joists resting on a ledger strip and nailed to beam.

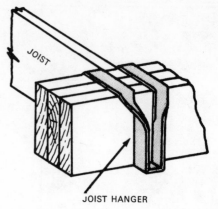

Joists positioned and held by metal hangers.

ledger: Narrow strips of wood nailed to the side of a beam to make a joist support.

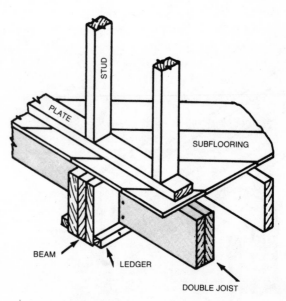

Double joist under a load bearing wall.

To frame a floor opening:

Openings in the floor for a chimney or stairway are framed as shown in the drawing.

1. Measure carefully to mark out the location of the opening. Mark the joists to be cut, using a pencil and try square. Allow for the thickness of a **double header** on each side of the opening.

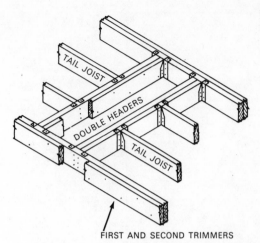

FIRST AND SECOND TRIMMERS

Framing members around a floor opening.

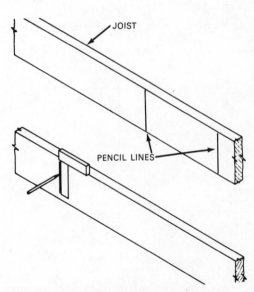

Marking the joists for a floor opening.

2. Nail a length of 19 mm by 89 mm strip across the undersides of the joists to be cut. These strips will support the joists until the headers can be nailed in place. Saw off the sections of the joists to make the opening. These joists are now called **tail joists** and those at either side of the opening are **trimmer joists**.

3. Cut the headers for the opening. Nail through the trimmer joists into the headers and through the headers into the tail joists, using 100 mm nails.

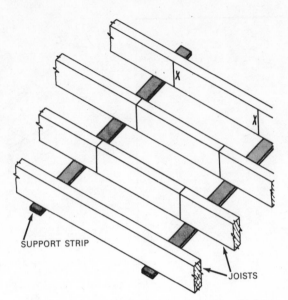

Temporary supports nailed to underside of joists.

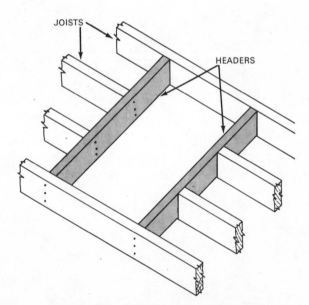

Opening headers positioned and nailed.

4. Double the headers by nailing the pieces in position as shown.

5. Since the trimmer joists must now support all loads placed over them as well as over the tail joists near the opening, they must also be doubled. These double joists are supported at both ends by the sill plate and the main beam.

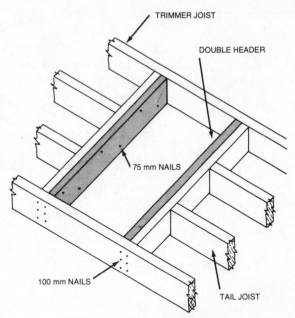

TRIMMER JOIST

DOUBLE HEADER

75 mm NAILS

100 mm NAILS

TAIL JOIST

Double headers nailed in place.

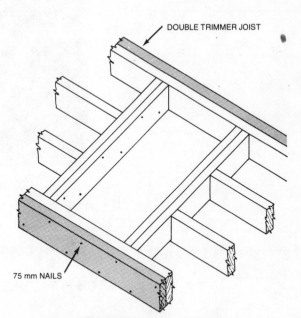

DOUBLE TRIMMER JOIST

75 mm NAILS

Double trimmer joists nailed in place.

6. If the tail joists and opening headers are longer than 1.2 m, they should be supported by metal joist hangers as well as by nails.

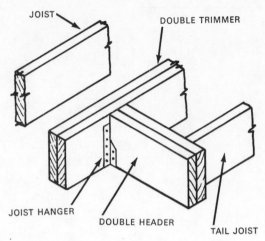

JOIST

DOUBLE TRIMMER

JOIST HANGER

DOUBLE HEADER

TAIL JOIST

Metal joist hanger used for extra support.

Metal joist hangers.

BRIDGING AND SUBFLOORING

WATCH FOR THESE WORDS

plumbing
mitre

subfloor
diagonally

HOW TO USE THESE WORDS

1. **Plumbing** is often installed between the floor joists.
2. The ends of cross bridging must be **mitre** cut to fit the joists.

3. Tongue-and-groove **subfloor** lumber is nailed **diagonally** across the floor frame.

FIND THE ANSWERS TO THESE QUESTIONS

1. What is the purpose of joist bridging?
2. Describe three types of approved bridging.
3. Why is cross bridging used more often than the other types even though it is more difficult to install?
4. Why are the lower ends of cross bridging left until the subfloor is installed before being nailed to the joists?
5. Why should lumber subflooring be laid diagonally over the floor joists?
6. State one objection to the use of square-edged lumber for subflooring.
7. What style of framing has subflooring laid crosswise to the floor joists?
8. In which direction should plywood sheets be installed for subflooring?
9. Describe a disadvantage of using square-edged plywood as subfloor material.

BRIDGING

To keep the floor joists from twisting and to transfer heavy loads from one joist to the others on either side, rows of supports called **bridging** must be installed. There must be one row of bridging for every 2.1 m of joist span. A building 8.53 m wide would need a row of bridging on each side of the main beam halfway from the main beam to the sill plate.

Courtesy Canadian Wood Council

Joist bridging.

plumbing: The pipe installed in the frame of a building to carry hot and cold water and provide drains for sinks, tubs, showers and toilets.

This bridging may consist of pieces of the joist material nailed in place between the joists.

The solid bridging shown is strong but makes the installation of **plumbing** and electrical wiring difficult. Another type of bridging is illustrated. Since the 19 mm by 89 mm strip is nailed to the underside of the joists, this method is never used where basement ceilings will be finished.

Cross bridging with 38 mm by 38 mm or 19 mm by 89 mm wood strips is the method most often used and is probably best for the job. However, it does take longer to install.

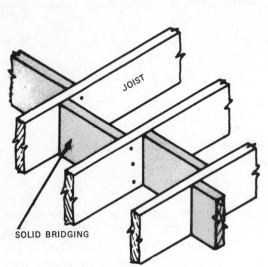

Stagger positioned solid bridging.

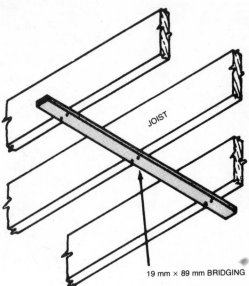

19 mm by 89 mm strip used as bridging

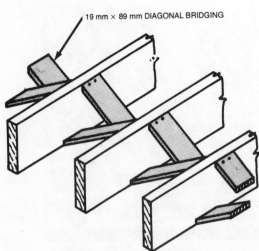

One size of cross bridging.

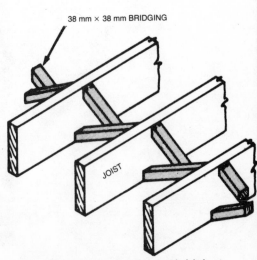

Another sample of cross bridging.

To cut and install cross bridging:

1. Cut a piece of scrap joist material to fit exactly between the floor joists at a point near the header.

2. Lay this piece diagonally on a length of bridging material as shown, and mark along the squared ends with a pencil.

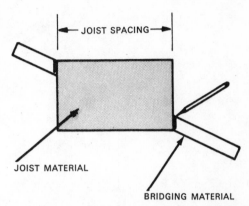

Using a piece of solid bridging to mark cross bridging.

3. Saw off the bridging material along the waste side of the pencil lines. The resulting piece should fit perfectly from the top of one joist to the bottom of the next. This piece is then the pattern for marking and cutting all of the cross bridging. Note that many lumber dealers sell precut cross bridging.

4. Since there will be two such pieces between each pair of joists, count the number of joist spaces and multiply by two to find the number of pieces for one row of bridging. If two or more rows of bridging are needed, multiply the number of pieces for one row by the correct number of rows.

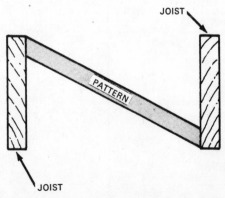

Checking the fit of the first piece of cross bridging.

mitre: To cut off pieces of wood on an angle of less than 90°

5. Use the cross bridging pattern to mark and cut the number of pieces needed.

The cross bridging pattern can also be used to make the cuts in a simple **mitre** box. Hold the bridging material with your hand while you make an end cut, then slide the material along to the proper length for the next cut.

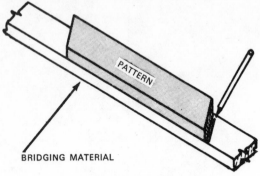

Using the bridging pattern.

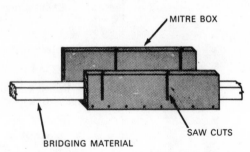

Simple mitre box used to cut bridging.

6. Start two 70 mm nails in each end of every piece of cross bridging.

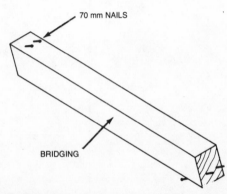

Prenailing each piece of cross bridging.

7. Measure the location of each row of bridging and mark the tops of the joists in a straight line from one end of the building to the other. Use a chalk line to do the marking.

8. Hold the bridging pieces in position and drive the nails at the top ends into the joists. Do not fasten the bottom ends to the joists until the subfloor has been nailed down. The joists will be in much better alignment once the subfloor is in place.

Nail bottom ends of cross bridging after the subfloor has been nailed in place.

SUBFLOORING

subfloor: A wood floor nailed on top of the floor framing to support the finish flooring.

diagonally: In a line from one corner to the opposite corner of a square or rectangle.

The **subfloor** is made of 19 mm lumber or 12.5 to 18.5 mm plywood nailed to the floor joists and headers. The finish flooring is later laid over this first rough floor.

When 19 mm lumber subflooring is used, the boards are laid **diagonally** over the floor joists and fastened with 65 mm nails. The whole floor framework is much more solidly braced against twisting when the subfloor is laid on this 45° angle than if it were laid cross-wise to the joists. The edge joints and cup warp will not interfere with finish flooring such as hardwood.

Square-edged lumber may be used for subflooring but it is not as rigid as tongue-and-groove material. The more rigid the subfloor, the fewer squeaks there will be in the finished floor.

Lumber subflooring laid diagonally.

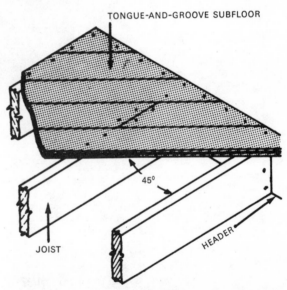

Diagonal installation of tongue-and-groove subflooring.

The only type of framework that uses lumber subflooring laid crosswise to the joists is the post-and-beam frame. However, in this case the tongue-and-groove material is 38 mm or 64 mm thick, and the floor joists are widely spaced beams. The drawing shows a post-and-beam subfloor. Note that unless the ends of the heavy subfloor boards are also tongue-and-groove, they must meet over one of the beams. Joints should not be side by side.

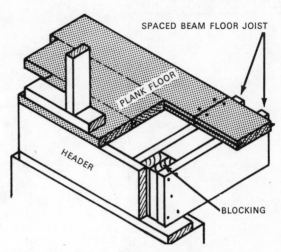

Plank subflooring on a post-and-beam frame.

To lay a diagonal subfloor:

The only difficulty in laying a diagonal subfloor is in starting the first board on the correct 45° angle.

1. Use a steel tape measure to measure 3 m from one corner along both headers. Mark these points with a pencil.

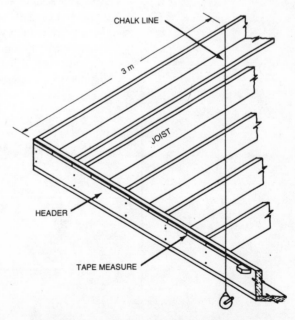

Locating the position of the first subfloor board.

2. Stretch a chalk line from one mark to the other and snap it to mark the joists.

3. Select a straight piece of subfloor lumber 4.88 m long and nail it in position along the chalk marks. Let the ends of the strip hang over the headers. When the floor is complete, these ends can be sawed off so that they are even with the outside of the headers.

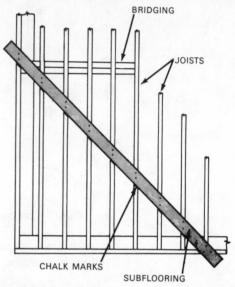

The first piece of subflooring nailed in place.

4. This first strip of subflooring is now positioned on a 45° angle to the floor joists. By working away from this piece in both directions all the subflooring will be laid at the correct angle. Where ends must be matched over a joist, use a combination square to mark the saw cuts. If some of the joists are warped, be sure to pull them into position for correct spacing before nailing the subfloor to them.

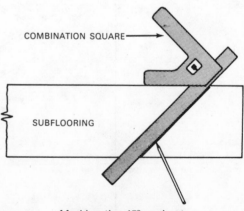

Marking the 45° end cuts.

When nailing plywood subflooring in position, be sure that the grain runs **across** the floor joists. If square-edged plywood is being used under a thin finish flooring, the edges of the panels must be supported by 38 mm by 89 mm cross pieces toenailed to the joists.

To avoid this extra labour and use of material, use tongue-and-groove plywood panels. Nails should be spaced 150 mm apart along panel edges and 300 mm apart along joists in the middle of the panels.

When all of the subfloor is nailed in place, the lower ends of the cross bridging can be nailed to the joists.

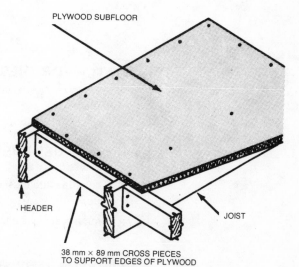

PLYWOOD SUBFLOOR

HEADER

JOIST

38 mm × 89 mm CROSS PIECES
TO SUPPORT EDGES OF PLYWOOD

Plywood subflooring. Tongue-and-groove edged sheets are self supporting between the joists.

CHAPTER 7

Wall Framing

WATCH FOR THESE WORDS

sole plate   partition

HOW TO USE THESE WORDS

1. The **sole plate** must be marked out to show the location of the wall studs.
2. Frame bracing is often needed in a **partition**.

FIND THE ANSWERS TO THESE QUESTIONS

1. List the names of the framing pieces that make up a wall frame.
2. What size of lumber is used for wall framing in a single-storey house?
3. How far apart should the wall studs be spaced?
4. Why must there be three studs at every corner?
5. When marking stud locations on the plates, why is an "X" marked beside the locating line?
6. How can the top plate be quickly marked out to be identical to the sole plate?
7. Find the length of wall studs needed for a wall 2700 mm high.
8. To what parts of the building frame should the sole plate be nailed when a wall section is raised into position?

In this discussion of wall framing, we will describe the type of framing used for a single-storey, platform frame house. The second-storey walls of a platform frame would be built in the same way as the first-storey walls. In braced and balloon frame construction, the walls are built in position instead of being stretched out on the platform and raised into position.

sole plate: The horizontal bottom part of a wall frame.

The **sole plate**, both top plates and the wall studs should all be made of the same size of 38 mm lumber. In single-storey construction, 38 mm by 89 mm lumber is usually used for partitions, while 38 mm by 140 mm lumber is used for outside walls. The outside walls are made thicker to provide better insulation. Preventing the loss of heat from a house is important since fuel is becoming scarce and costly. Wall studs are usually spaced 400 mm apart. If light loads will be supported, 600 mm spacing is acceptable. Where loads will be heavy, wall studs may be spaced 300 mm apart. Of course, more studs make the wall frame stronger, but they also increase its cost.

A wall frame being moved into position.

MARKING OUT THE PLATES

Place straight lengths of 38 mm lumber around the subfloor platform, flush with the outside edge. Drive a few 90 mm nails through each piece to hold it in position for marking out the stud locations. Do not drive these nails in all the way because this sole plate will later be turned on edge to build the wall frame.

At each corner, mark the location of the studs that will form the corner posts. The most commonly used style of corner post is made up of three studs and spacer blocks nailed together with 75 mm nails. Corner studs must be placed so that both inside and outside wall coverings can be nailed in place at the corner.

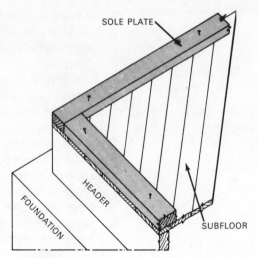

The sole plates in position around the platform.

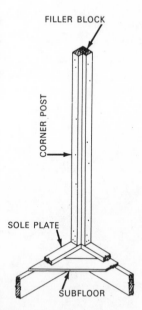

The construction of a corner post with three studs. Notice the scrap pieces used for filler blocks.

The sole plate should be marked at each corner. Use a combination square to mark the location lines across the plate, and place a pencilled "X" where the end of each stud will be nailed.

COMBINATION SQUARE

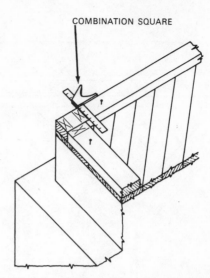

Marking the position of the corner post studs.

Measure 400 mm from the outside of each corner along the sole plates. This point is the centre of the first stud along each wall. Mark the stud locations as shown in the drawing.

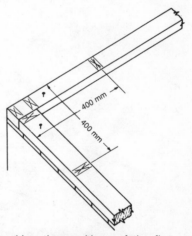

Locating and marking the positions of the first studs along each wall.

Hold a steel tape measure at the first wall stud and mark the sole plate every 400 mm. Square a line across the plate at these points, and place an "X" on the side nearest the first stud. This "X" marks the side of the line on which the wall stud will be installed.

From the building blueprint, find the location of each inside **partition** wall. Carefully measure and mark the sole plate where these walls will meet the outside wall. No matter how close a partition comes to a regularly spaced wall stud, two studs must be positioned as shown in the drawing.

partition: A wall that separates one room from another.

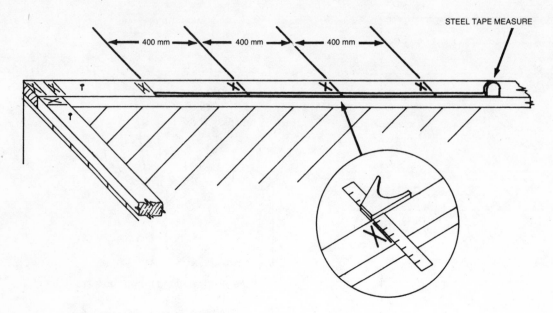

Marking the stud positions every 400 mm beginning at the first stud.

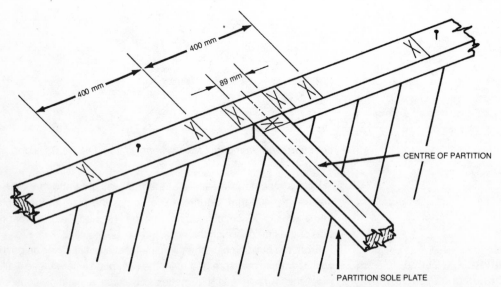

Wall studs at a partition must be positioned to form a corner on both sides of the partition.

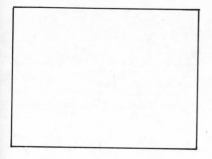

LAYING OUT WINDOW AND DOOR OPENINGS

Use the building blueprints to find the location and rough opening width of the doors and windows in the outer walls. Mark these openings on the sole plate. Note that window and door openings are often located on the blueprints by their centre points.

The studs are doubled at both sides of window and door openings but the inner studs do not run to the top plate. Mark their locations with a "C" for **cripple stud**.

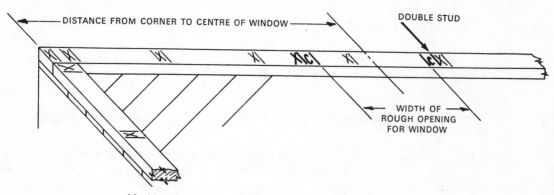

Marking the double stud positions for a window opening.

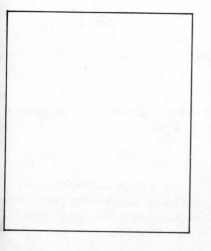

LAYING OUT THE TOP PLATE

When all of the stud locations have been marked on the sole plate, pull out the nails holding one length of plate and place this plate beside a piece of 38 mm lumber that is exactly the same width and length. Lay a combination square across both pieces and mark the stud locations on the second piece. This length of material is then identical to the sole plate and becomes the top wall plate.

The studs should now be cut to the correct length, and this section of wall should be assembled and raised into position. As soon as it has been nailed and braced in position, pull the nails from the next piece of sole plate and lay out a length of top plate to match it. By building the walls one section at a time until the outside wall framing is complete, the work is kept organized and you will make fewer mistakes.

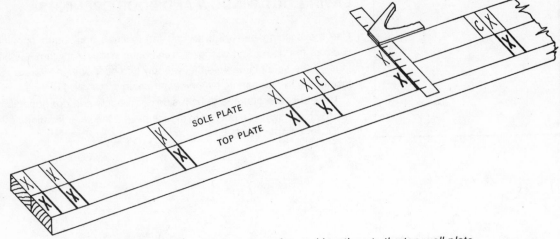

Using a combination square to transfer stud locations to the top wall plate.

MEASURING AND CUTTING THE WALL STUDS

Of couse, it is important that all of the full-length wall studs are exactly the same length. Therefore, you should measure and cut the first stud and use it as a pattern to mark all of the others. Mark it in **large** black letters. Another method is to construct a simple mitre box as shown in the photograph.

Lumber dealers have precut wall studs for all standard wall heights. These save time and reduce waste.

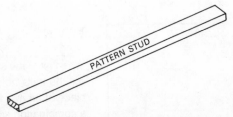

A carefully measured and cut wall stud marked for use as a pattern for the others.

The length of the pattern stud can be found by subtracting the thicknesses of the sole plate and doubled top plate from the height of the wall marked on the building plans. For example, if the height of the wall is to be 2400 mm, the length of the studs will be:

$2400 - (38 + 38 + 38)$

$= 2400 - 114$

$= 2286$ mm

Count the number of full-length studs needed. Mark them, then cut them from straight 38 mm lumber.

Using a power saw and mitre box to cut the stud lengths. The box is made of two pieces of plywood nailed to the sides of a long 38 mm by 89 mm with a stop block nailed to the other end.

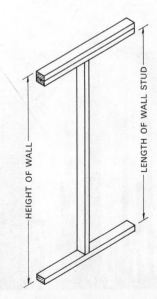

Note that stud length is not the same as wall height.

ASSEMBLING A CORNER POST

There are usually many short lengths of 38 mm lumber around a building site, especially after the studs have been cut to length. Position three of these pieces between two full-length studs, and nail through the studs into these blocks with 75 mm nails.

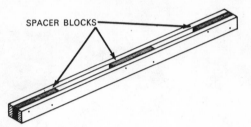

SPACER BLOCKS

Using short lengths of 38 mm *by* 89 mm *to space corner studs.*

The third stud in the post assembly is not nailed in place at this time. It is first made a part of the adjoining wall. When both walls have been raised, they are joined at the corner.

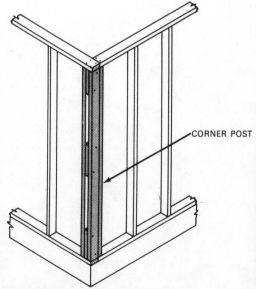

CORNER POST

The appearance of a corner post.

BUILDING A WALL SECTION

Set the sole plate and top plate on edge on the subfloor, and place the studs in position between them. When all of the full-length studs are in position, drive three 90 mm nails through the plates into the end of each stud. Because the wall section pictured has no door or window opening to frame, it may be lifted into position as soon as the studs are all nailed in place.

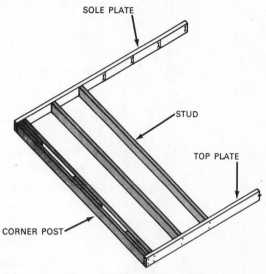

Nailing the wall studs in position between the plates.

Use a level to make sure the wall is vertical, and brace it in position with one or more lengths of 19 mm by 89 mm lumber.

Drive 100 mm nails through the sole plate into the header and floor joists. The wall section is now complete except for the permanent bracing and the double top plate. These members are added when all of the wall sections are in place.

A wall frame being held by temporary braces.

WALL OPENINGS AND CORNER BRACING

WATCH FOR THESE WORDS

lintel   dado
cripple

HOW TO USE THESE WORDS

1. **Cripple** studs support the **lintels** above door and window openings.
2. Let-in bracing is fitted tightly into **dado** cuts in the studs.

FIND THE ANSWERS TO THESE QUESTIONS

1. Why must the size of window lintels be increased over wide openings?
2. Why are rough window sills often doubled?
3. List three standard door heights.
4. How far above the subfloor should the lintel be positioned for a standard 2030 mm door?
5. How wide should the rough opening be for an 810 mm door?
6. What is a partition?
7. To what part of the building frame should the sole plate of the partitions be nailed?
8. What tool is used to plumb a partition?
9. Why must the double top plate overlap at all corner and partition joints?
10. When is it necessary to install extra frame bracing?
11. Name two styles of frame bracing.
12. Which style of bracing is the strongest?
13. Why might it be necessary to brace partition studs?

FRAMING A WINDOW OPENING

Rough openings for windows are pictured below. The wall studs are doubled on both sides of the opening. The inner studs support the **lintel**. The size of material used for the lintel depends on the width of the opening and the load that will have to be supported. However, the solid style is often used for all of the window openings in a house

lintel: A horizontal part of a wall frame that supports the load over an opening such as a door or window.

because it saves the time required to cut and install short cripple studs above the lintel. Two 286 mm pieces are used over very wide openings.

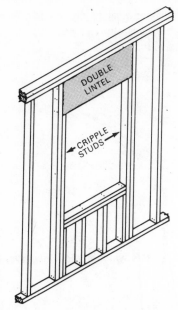

Framing a window opening using a solid lintel.

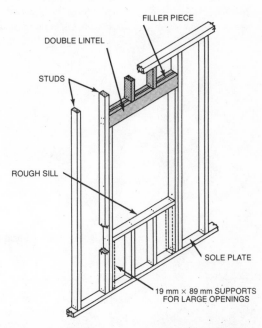

Short cripple studs installed over a light window lintel.

A framed opening for a window.

The lintel members must have a piece of 12.5 mm plywood between them so that the total thickness will be the same as the width of the wall studs. A 140 mm thick wall will need 64 mm spacer blocks between the lintel pieces. The rough window sill may be made of one length of 38 mm lumber, but a double sill is stronger and provides a larger nailing area for the finish window trim.

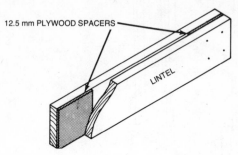

12.5 mm PLYWOOD SPACERS

LINTEL

Plywood spacers make the lintel the same width as the wall studs.

FRAMING A DOOR OPENING

The height of a rough door opening is established by the height of the standard door being framed plus the thickness of the finish door frame and the finish flooring. Standard heights of doors are 1980 mm, 2030 mm, and 2080 mm. Some larger houses have 2130 mm front doors to suit the size of the building.

Using an 810 mm by 2030 mm door as an example, and allowing 50 mm for the thickness of finish flooring and finish door frame, the lintel will be 2080 mm above the subfloor. When this height is established, mark and cut one of the **cripple** studs to length, and use it as a pattern to mark the studs for all door openings of this size.

The width of door openings is also controlled by the standard door size. Standard widths are 760 mm, 810 mm, 860 mm, or 910 mm. In partitions, the rough opening should be 50 mm wider than the door. This allows for the thickness of the finish frame and leaves 6 mm on both sides for straightening and squaring the finish frame. As in framing a window opening, the lintel may be solid to the plate or have short cripple studs from lintel to plate.

cripple: Any framing piece that is cut shorter than full-length pieces of the same type.

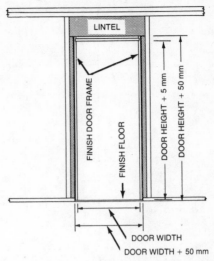

LINTEL

FINISH DOOR FRAME

FINISH FLOOR

DOOR HEIGHT + 5 mm

DOOR HEIGHT + 50 mm

DOOR WIDTH

DOOR WIDTH + 50 mm

Determining the height and width of a rough door frame in a partition.

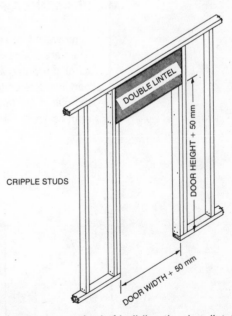

DOUBLE LINTEL

DOOR HEIGHT + 50 mm

CRIPPLE STUDS

DOOR WIDTH + 50 mm

A common method of building the door lintel.

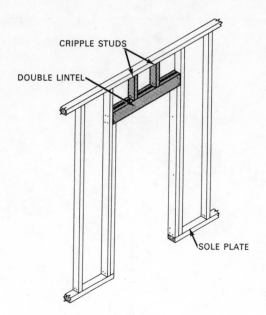

Another method of building the door lintel.

FRAMING A PARTITION

Inner walls that separate one room from another are called partitions. They are built using the same methods as for the outer walls. When all of the outer wall sections are nailed and braced in position, the partition sole plates are cut and tacked in place with a few nails. The top plates are laid beside the sole plates, and the stud locations are marked on both pieces at the same time.

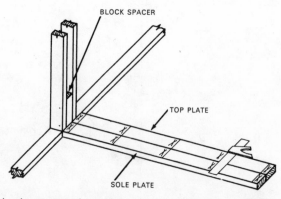

Laying out stud positions on the plates for a partition.

As the plates for each partition are marked out, turn them on edge and nail the studs in position with 90 mm nails. Raise the partition and nail the sole plate to the subfloor with 100 mm nails driven through the flooring and into the joists.

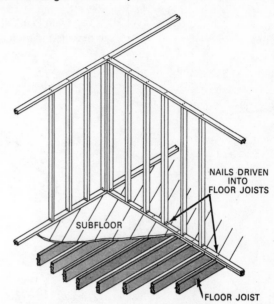

The sole plate should be nailed to the floor joists, not just to the subfloor.

Hold a level against the edge of the first partition stud, and move the partition until it is plumb. Drive 90 mm nails through this stud into the blocking between the outer wall studs.

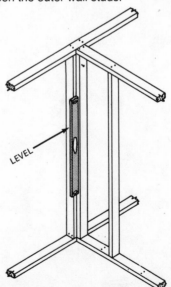

Using a long level to make certain the partition is vertical before being nailed in place.

When all of the partitions have been built and nailed in place, the top plates are doubled by nailing lengths of 38 mm lumber to the first plate with 75 mm nails spaced about 600 mm apart. Double the top plates of the partitions first so that each partition is tied to the outer wall.

Top plate joints should overlap at the corners and along the walls to provide the greatest possible frame strength.

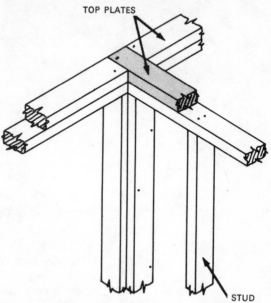

The double top plate of a partition should lap over the outside wall plate.

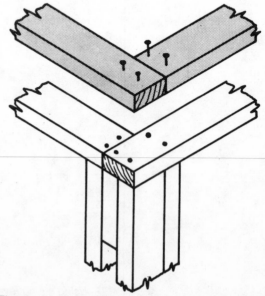

The double top plates must overlap at the corners.

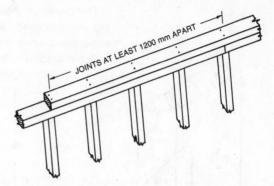

Joints in the double top plate should not come together.

FRAME BRACING

When the frame will be covered with wood sheathing laid at a 45° angle or with plywood sheathing, there is little need for extra frame bracing. However, when fiberboard or gypsum board is used for sheathing, either **let-in** or **cut-in bracing** should be installed at every corner. Both types of bracing are installed at a 45° angle. Where possible, the bracing should run from the top plate to the bottom plate.

Let-in bracing must be installed before the sheathing is nailed in place. The studs are marked and **dadoed** to receive a 19 mm by 89 mm strip to form a let-in brace flush with the outside of the frame.

dado: A wide, shallow cross cut in wood.

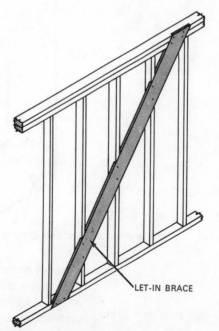

LET-IN BRACE

Let-in brace even with the edges of the studs.

The drawings show how the studs are marked for dados. Break out
the wood between the saw cuts with a wood chisel, and use the
same tool to smooth the bottom of the dado.

Cut-in bracing is installed after the sheathing has been nailed on. It

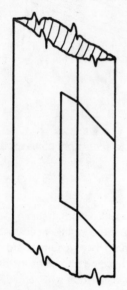

A stud marked for a let-in brace.

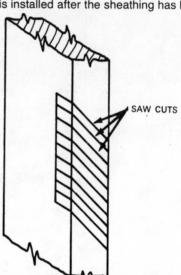

SAW CUTS

Make saw cuts about 18 mm *apart.*

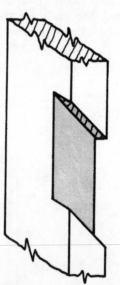

Use a wide wood chisel to remove the waste from each dado.

depends on the holding power of nails for its bracing strength.

Mark the brace location on the wall studs by holding a straight
length of lumber against the wall and marking along its edge. Each
piece of bracing may then be held along these marks, carefully
marked, cut and then nailed in place.

This method of bracing takes more time to install, is comparatively weak and makes the installation of electric wiring more difficult. However, it is a way of using the many short lengths of 38 mm by 89 mm lumber that might otherwise be wasted.

Partitions are sometimes braced horizontally in order to prevent the studs from bowing, and to create firestops.

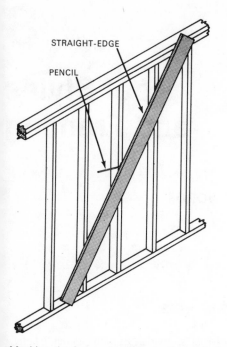

Marking the brace position on the wall studs.

Cut-in bracing.

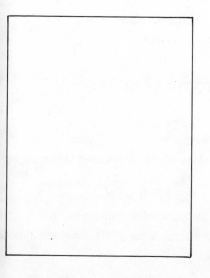

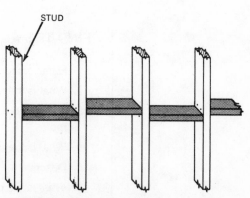

Horizontal bracing installed in a partition.

CHAPTER 8

Roof Styles
and Framing

WATCH FOR THESE WORDS

run	rise
span	overhang
pitch	fascia

HOW TO USE THESE WORDS

1. Rafter **run** is one-half the roof **span** in most house construction.
2. One way to describe the **pitch** of a roof is to compare its **rise** to its run.
3. The **overhang** of a roof is a horizontal measurement.
4. A **fascia** board trims the edge of a roof.

FIND THE ANSWERS TO THESE QUESTIONS

1. Name six roof styles that are used in house building.
2. What is the function of the rafter in roof construction?
3. Name and describe four kinds of roof rafters used to frame a hip roof.
4. What is the function of the ridge board and the collar ties?
5. Describe the meaning of roof span, rafter run and roof rise.
6. What is the pitch of a roof that has a rise of 3000 mm and a span of 12 000 mm?

7. What is the pitch of a roof that has a rise of 2000 mm and a run of 5000 mm?
8. Use the rafter tables on a Stanley square to find the length of a common rafter for a roof with 1 to 2 pitch and a span of 10.
9. Use the rafter tables on a Frederickson square to find the length per unit of run of the following rafters:
    (a) 100 mm rise over 250 mm run
    (b) 250 mm rise over 250 mm run
    (c) 150 mm rise over 250 mm run
10. What is the total length of each of the above rafters if their total run is 4000 mm?
11. Why should slightly crowned edges of rafters always be face up?
12. On a piece of 38 mm by 89 mm lumber that is 2 m long, mark out a common rafter for a 1000 mm run and a rise of 150 mm in 250 mm. The overhang is 250 mm and the ridge board is 38 mm lumber.
13. Use a hand cross-cut saw to make the cuts in this rafter.

Of the six styles of roofs pictured here, the **gable roof** is by far the most commonly used. Many ranch-style houses are built with **hip roofs** to add to the long, low appearance. **Gambrel roofs** were once popular for one-and-a-half storey houses and are often used today in barn construction. The **shed roof** and **flat roof** are becoming more popular each year. The **mansard roof** is an older style now used to give two-storey and split-level homes a lower roof line.

The style of the roof sets the overall style of the building. Because the roof is the most distinctive feature of the house, everyone has a favourite style.

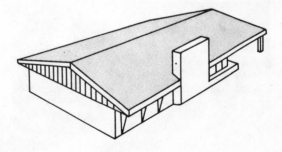

Gable roofs.

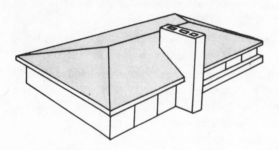

Hip roofs, which are widely known as cottage roofs.

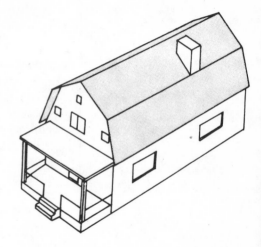

Gambrel roofs.

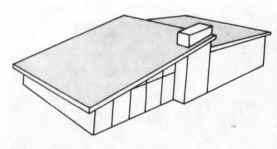

Shed roofs.

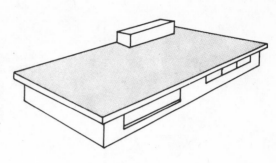

Flat roofs.

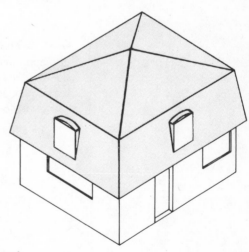

Mansard roofs.

The roof frame is quite complicated. In fact, it is probably the most difficult part of a house to build. Therefore, you should study the following words and phrases used by carpenters to describe roof framing. The drawing shows the location of the roof framing members.

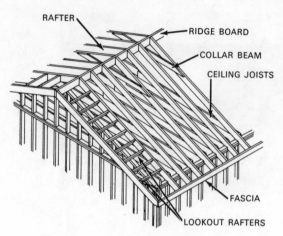

The framing members of a gable roof.

Rafters are the framing pieces that form the shape of the roof and support the roof sheathing and shingles. The size of each rafter depends upon the span and pitch of the roof. Rafter size also depends on how far apart the rafters are spaced. In most cases, 38 mm by 140 mm lumber or 38 mm by 184 mm lumber is used. It is spaced 400 mm or 600 mm apart. Rafters that extend from the wall plate to the ridge board are called **common rafters**. **Hip rafters** extend from a corner of the plate to the ridge board on hip roofs.

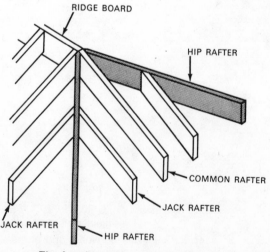

The framing at the ends of a hip roof.

Valley rafters form the joint between two roofs and also extend from the plate, but often reach only to the ridge of one of the roofs. All rafters that extend from the wall plate to hip rafters or from the ridge board to valley rafters are called **jack rafters**.

The **ridge board** is a length of 19 mm or 38 mm lumber used to form the top edge of the roof and hold the rafters solidly in place so that their top edges are straight and level with one another.

Collar ties are cross pieces nailed to each pair of rafters to strengthen them.

The **fascia** or facer board is made of 19 mm or 38 mm lumber nailed to the lower ends of the rafters to form the edge of the roof and to hide the ends of the rafters.

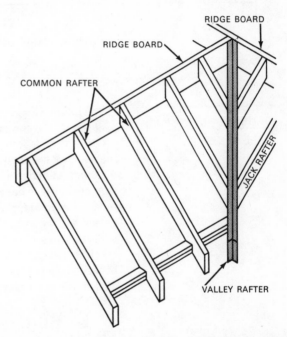

The method of framing the joint between two roofs of equal height.

run = ½ × span

The **span** of a roof is the distance from the outside of a wall plate to the outside of the opposite wall plate. It is the width of the building frame.

The **run** of a rafter is the horizontal distance from the outside of the wall plate on which the rafter is resting to the centre of the ridge board. Since the ridge board is usually positioned above the centre of the building, the run of each rafter is **exactly half the span** of the roof.

The **rise** of a roof is the vertical distance from the top of the rafter at the wall plates to the top of the rafter at the ridge board.

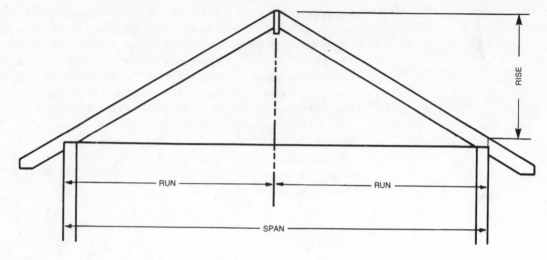

An illustration of roof building terms.

$$pitch = \frac{rise}{span}$$

The **pitch** of a roof is its **slope**, which may be steep or low. Even fla roofs have a slight slope for drainage.

One way to describe the pitch of a roof is to express it as a fraction the rise over the span. For example, a roof with a 3000 mm rise and 9000 mm span has a pitch of $^{3000}/_{9000}$, or a $^1/_3$ pitch.

Another way to describe the pitch of a roof is to show it in the form c a right-angled triangle drawn above the rafter or roof drawings in th blueprints. The vertical and horizontal sides of this triangle are draw to dimension and the third side follows the roof slope. When reading the pitch symbol, the vertical dimension is always read first, then th horizontal dimension. For example, a roof with a low slope could hav a pitch of 1 to 12, and a steeper roof could slope 1 to 2.

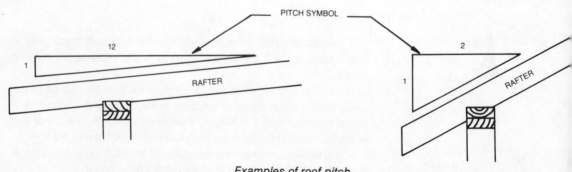

Examples of roof pitch.

If the pitch of a roof is 1 to 1 or less, then the vertical dimension is always 1. If the pitch of a roof is steeper than 1 to 1, the horizontal dimension is always 1.

When using a framing square to mark out a rafter, the carpenter will need to use this pitch information.

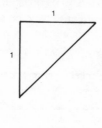
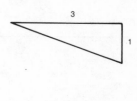

3 to 1, 1 to 1, and 1 to 3 roof pitches.

MARKING AND CUTTING A COMMON RAFTER

The **framing square** pictured below is much like the rise and run of a rafter if you can imagine the rafter stretching from the tip of the body to the tip of the tongue of the square. When the framing square is used to mark out a rafter, it is placed in this way. Of course, the square will not be large enough to extend from end to end of a full-size rafter, and the pitch of the roof will not always match the shape of the square.

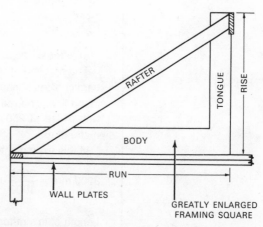

The body of this square measures rafter run while the tongue measures the rise.

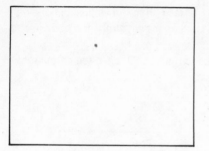

FINDING RAFTER LENGTH

Each framing square has a set of **rafter tables** on one side of its bod
To find rafter length, you must use the line of numbers that is marke
"Length of Common Rafters."

Since the run of rafters changes from building to building, it ha
been necessary to establish a standard unit of run. The tables on th
Stanley square are based on a unit of run of 1 m.

	40	30	20	10	500	90	80	70	60	40	30	20	10	400	90
mm RISE PER METRE RUN									250			300		400	
mm LENGTH COMMON RAFTERS PER METRE RUN									1031			1044		1077	
mm LENGTH HIP OR VALLEY PER METRE RUN									1436			1446		1470	
mm DIFFERENCE IN LENGTH OF JACKS, 400 mm centres								412				418		431	
mm DIFFERENCE IN LENGTH OF JACKS, 600 mm centres								618				626		646	
FOR SIDE CUT OF JACKS USE OPPOSITE 200 mm line								194				192		186	
FOR SIDE CUT OF HIP OR VALLEY USE OPPOSITE								197	200 mm line			196		193	
	500	90	80	70	60	50	40	30	20	10	400	90	80	70	60

Part of the rafter tables on a Stanley square.

Example:

Using this square, find the length of a common rafter for a roof with 1 t
4 pitch and a run of 3000 mm.

First, change the pitch to show the rise per metre of run. This is don
by expressing the pitch as a fraction, then multiplying it by 1000 mr
(which equals 1 m).

¼ × 1000 = 250 mm

The rafter will have a 250 mm rise over every metre of run.

The first line of rafter tables on the square shows a series of stan
dard choices of rise per metre of run. Note that the number 250 is firs
in the line. The number 1031 directly below 250 means that a rafte
with a rise of 250 mm per metre of run will measure 1031 mm pe
metre of run.

In this example, the run of the common rafter is 3000 mm.

$$3000 \text{ mm} = \frac{3000}{1000} \text{ m} = 3 \text{ m}$$

Length of this rafter from wall plate to ridge board:

3 × 1031 = 3093 mm

overhang: The horizontal distance from the outside of the support wall to the edge of a roof.

The additional length of rafter for the **overhang** may be found by multiplying the amount of overhang in metres of run by the rafter length per metre of run.

In this example, the overhang is 600 mm.

$$600 \text{ mm} = \frac{600}{1000} \text{ m} = 0.6 \text{ m}$$

Length of rafter over this distance:

$$0.6 \times 1031 = 618.6 \text{ mm}$$

Add the length of the rafter to the overhang length to find the total rafter length:

$$3093 + 618.6 = 3711.6 \text{ mm}$$

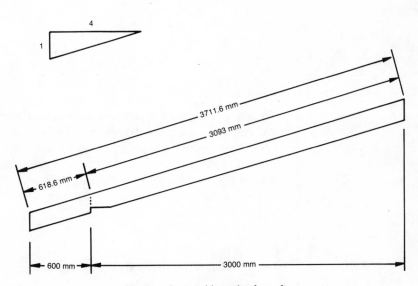

Finding the total length of a rafter.

A metric framing square has recently been developed in Canada by Paul Frederickson. It has been inspected and approved by the Canadian Metric Commission.

The rafter tables on the Frederickson square are based on a 250 mm unit of run. If this square is adopted as our official standard, in the future we may find the pitch symbol on building blueprints showing the rise in 250 mm of run.

Part of the rafter tables on the Frederickson square.

Example:

To find the length of a common rafter with a pitch of 100 mm to 250 mm, first locate the 100 mm mark on the outside scale on the body of the Frederickson square. Read the number below it on the line marked "Length of Com. per Unit Run." This number is 269.3 and means that the rafter length in 250 mm of run will be 269.3 mm.

This common rafter has a run of 3000 mm.

$$\frac{3000}{250} = 12 \text{ units of run}$$

Length of this rafter from wall plate to ridge board:

$12 \times 269.3 = 3231.6$ mm

The additional length of rafter to provide the 600 mm of overhang may be found by first dividing the overhang length by 250:

$$\frac{600}{250} = 2.4 \text{ units of run}$$

Length of overhang:

$2.4 \times 269.3 = 646.3$ mm

Total rafter length:

$3231.6 + 646.3 = 3877.9$ mm

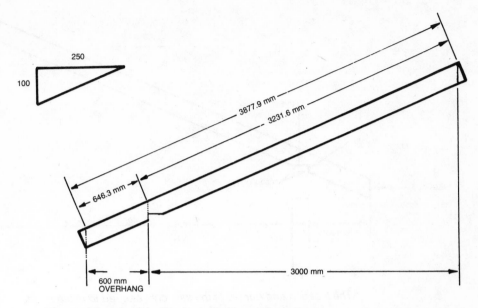

The total length of a rafter includes the roof overhang.

CUTTING THE RAFTER

The next drawing shows the four saw cuts that must be accurately made to provide exact fits at the ridge board and wall plate. Once you have found the length of the rafter, carefully follow these steps in laying out the cuts.

The rafter shown in the example above will also be used for this layout. It has a 100 mm in 250 mm pitch and a 3000 mm run. This first rafter will be a pattern from which the others will be marked and cut. Choose the straightest length of rafter material in the pile. The crown of any slight warp should be the top edge of the rafter.

To mark out a rafter (using the Frederickson square):

1. Lay the rafter material flat across two sawhorses or benches. Place the framing square in the position shown so that the rise per unit of run on the tongue and the 250 mm mark on the body are even with the top edge of the rafter. Draw a pencil along the tongue to mark the **ridge plumb cut**.

2. Use a steel measuring tape to measure the length of the rafter from the top of the plumb cut along the top edge of the rafter. Mark the length and place the framing square as in the drawing so that the rise per unit of run is on the length mark. Draw a pencil along the tongue to mark the **plumb seat cut**.

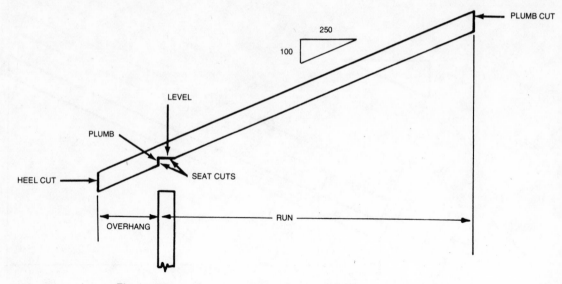

The location and names of the saw cuts needed to make a rafter.

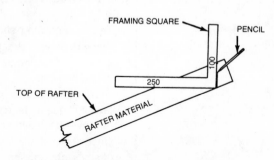

Marking the ridge plumb cut.

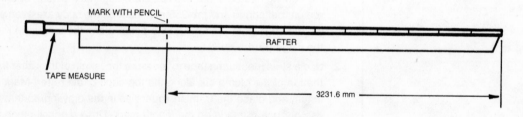

Measure the length of the rafter.

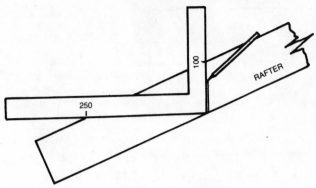

Mark the seat plumb cut.

3. The **level seat cut** should fit the width of the wall plate. The wall plate is either 89 mm or 140 mm wide. Hold the square along the plumb seat cut mark and move it up or down until the correct mark on the body of the square is even with the bottom edge of the rafter. Mark the level cut with a pencil as shown.

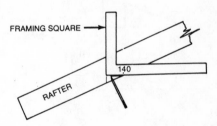

Marking the level seat cut to fit a 140 mm top plate.

4. Measure the overhang length of the rafter as shown.
5. Place the framing square at this mark and mark the **heel cut**.

Where the rafter material is 140 mm in width or more, a **level heel cut** must be made to reduce the height of the rafter end so that it may be covered with a **narrow fascia**. If the height of the rafter end is not reduced, the fascia will be too wide to be attractive. In order to form a narrow fascia, measure along the heel cut and mark a level cut with the framing square as shown. The illustration shows a heel height of 120 mm. A 140 mm fascia would be used in this case.

fascia: A board nailed to the heels of the rafters to form the edge of the roof.

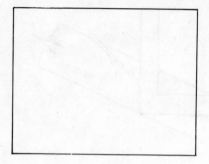

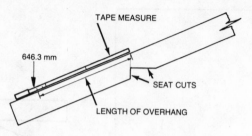

Measuring the length of rafter overhang.

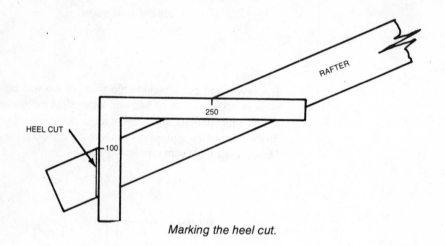

Marking the heel cut.

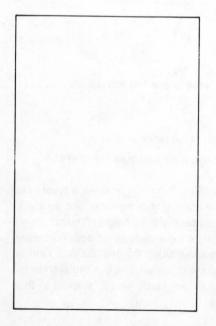

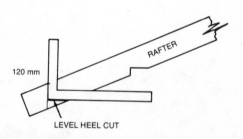

Marking the level heel cut.

6. This rafter is now marked out to give the correct rise over the total run. Since the run of a rafter is measured to the centre of the ridge board, half of the ridge board thickness should be removed from each rafter. Hold a square along the plumb cut mark and measure half of the ridge board thickness. Mark the new plumb cut. The thickness of the rough fascia may also be removed from the heel of the rafter.

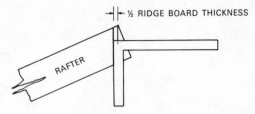

—|‖— ½ RIDGE BOARD THICKNESS

Marking the allowance for ridge board thickness.

7. When all of the cuts have been marked on the rafter and you have checked to make sure they are correct, carefully saw along the waste side of the lines with a hand cross-cut saw. Mark this rafter as a pattern, and use it to mark the cuts on all of the rafters needed.

PATTERN

Using the pattern rafter to mark the remaining rafters.

ROOF FRAMING IN THE IMPERIAL SYSTEM

Remember that the pitch of a roof is its slope, which may be steep or low. The pitch of the roof is expressed as a fraction, the rise over the span. For example, the pitch of a roof with an 8 ft. rise and a 24 ft. span is described as having a pitch of $^8/_{24}$ or $^1/_3$.

The pitch of a roof is also expressed as the amount of rise in 12 in. of rafter run. For example, a rafter that has a total rise of 5 ft. over a 10 ft. run has a pitch of 6 in. in 12 in. This often appears on the blueprints as a small triangle over the rafter detail as shown below.

In the inch-foot system, the roof pitch is therefore expressed as so many inches of rise per 12 in. of run. Find the number of inches of rise on the tongue of a framing square and 12 in. on the body. Measure the distance between these two numbers. This distance is the length of the rafter in 12 in. of run. The length of common rafter per foot of run may also be found in the first line of the rafter tables on the framing square.

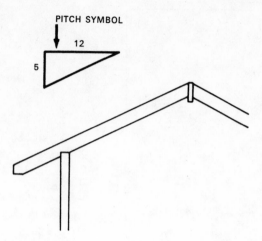

A blueprint symbol used to show the pitch of a roof.

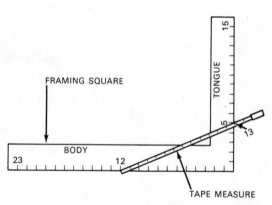

Finding the length of a rafter per foot of run.

Example:

The roof drawing below shows a rise of 5 in. Using a framing square the length of rafter per foot of run is measured as 13 in. The rafter run in this example is 10 ft. The length of the rafter can now be found by multiplying its length per foot of run by the number of feet in the run. Length of the rafter from wall plate to ridge board:

10 × 13 = 130 in. = 10 ft. 10 in.

When the rafter is to hang over the wall frame, this additional length may be found by multiplying the amount of overhang in feet by the length per foot of run. The overhang for the rafter in this example is 2 ft.
Increase in the length of the rafter:

2 × 13 = 26 in. = 2 ft. 2 in.

Add the length of the rafter to the overhang length to find the total rafter length:

10 ft. 10 in. + 2 ft. 2 in. = 13 ft.

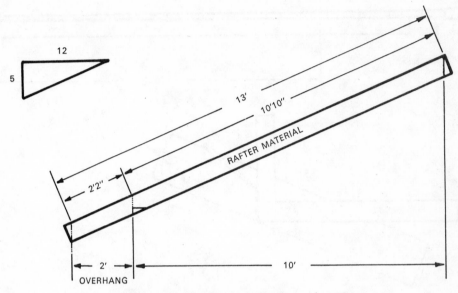

The total length of a rafter includes the roof overhang.

To mark out a rafter:

1. Lay the rafter material flat across two sawhorses or benches and place the framing square in the position shown, so that the rise per foot of run on the tongue and the 12 in. mark on the body are even with the top edge of the rafter. Draw a pencil along the tongue to mark the ridge plumb cut.

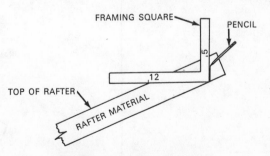

Marking the ridge plumb cut.

2. Use a steel measuring tape to measure the length of the rafter from the top of the plumb cut along the top edge of the rafter. Mark the length and place the framing square as shown below so that the rise per foot of run is on the length mark. Draw a pencil along the tongue to mark the plumb seat cut.

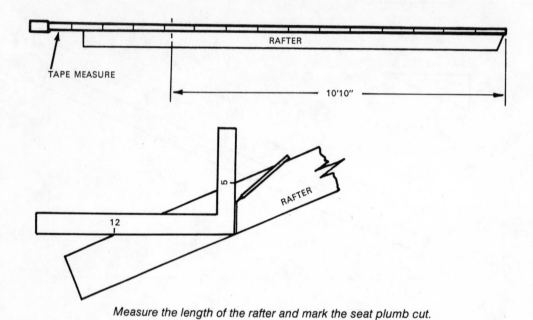

Measure the length of the rafter and mark the seat plumb cut.

3. The level seat cut should fit the width of the wall. The wall plate is 4 in. wide in most cases. Hold the square along the plumb seat cut mark and move it up or down until the 4 in. mark on the body of the square is even with the bottom edge of the rafter. Mark the level cut with a pencil as shown.

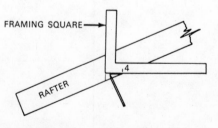

Marking the level seat cut to fit a 4 in. top plate.

4. Measure the overhang length of the rafter as shown.

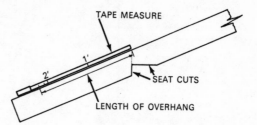

Measuring the length of rafter overhang.

5. Place the framing square at this mark as shown below, and mark the heel cut.

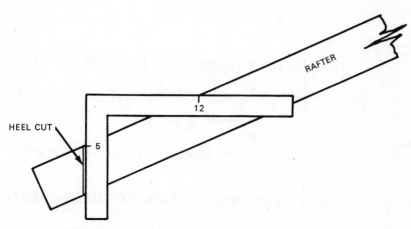

Marking the heel cut.

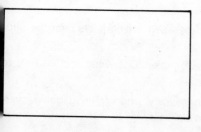

Where the rafter material is 6 in. in width or more, a level heel cut must be made to reduce the height of the rafter end so that it may be covered with a narrow fascia. (If the height of the rafter end is not reduced, the fascia will be too wide.) In order to make a narrow fascia, measure along the heel cut and mark a level cut with the framing square as shown. The illustration shows a heel height of 5 in. A 6 in. fascia would be used in this case.

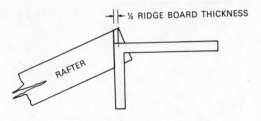

Marking the level heel cut.

FRAMING A CEILING

WATCH FOR THESE WORDS

attic	prefabricate
ventilator	timber

HOW TO USE THESE WORDS

1. A **ventilator** should be installed at each end of an **attic** space.
2. It is possible to **prefabricate** sets of truss rafters for any style of roof.
3. A length of solid **timber** may be used as a beam.

FIND THE ANSWERS TO THESE QUESTIONS

1. What determines the size of material used for ceiling joists?
2. What is the usual joist spacing for celings?
3. How might joists be supported in the middle when there is no support partition?
4. Describe two methods of joining pairs of joists over the support partition.
5. Why is solid bridging used between ceiling joists over the support partition?
6. When marking the length of gable studs, what tool is used to make sure the stud is vertical?
7. Why are lookout rafters necessary when framing gable overhangs that are greater than 300 mm?

8. List five advantages of truss roof framing over the ordinary joist and rafter method.
9. Name three types of ridge beam used in post-and-beam construction.
10. Suggest a reason why houses with post-and-beam frames are usually less expensive to build than conventional houses.

CEILING JOISTS

The size of lumber used for ceiling joists depends on their spacing, the distance they must span and the load they must carry. When you study the blueprints for various houses, you will notice how the joist sizes vary according to the building style.

In one-and-a-half storey and two-storey frame construction, the first-storey ceiling joists are also the second-storey floor joists and will probably be the same size as or one size smaller than those used to frame the first floor.

attic: The space between the ceiling joists and the rafters of a building.

Ceiling joists framing an **attic** area not used for storage or living space may be of lighter material or spaced farther apart. Just as in floor framing, the ceiling joists are usually spaced 400 mm apart, although 300 mm or 600 mm on centre may be used in some cases.

In flat roof construction, the ceiling joists also serve as rafters. The built-up roofing material is very heavy. In some areas, snow piles up a large weight on the roof. Therefore joists for flat roofs must be large and strong.

The heavy framing used for flat roofs.

FRAMING THE CEILING

Ceiling joists extend across the width of a building and are supported by the side wall plates and by one or more partitions.

A partition running the full length of the building is not always on the blueprint. In this case, the joists must be framed into the side of a beam with metal joist hangers to give support over these open spaces.

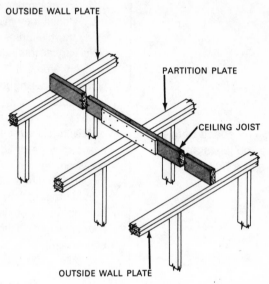

Ceiling joists resting on the wall and partition plates.

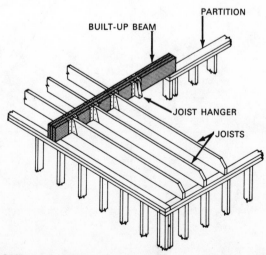

Ceiling joists framed into a beam over an open area.

Most buildings are too wide for a single length of joist material to span them. Joists may be either lapped and nailed over a partition, or butted with a 19 mm thick strap nailed to the sides.

The ends of the joists will be nailed to the sides of the rafters as well as to the wall plates. Therefore, the butted and strapped method of fastening the joists together is preferred. It prevents one or both of the joists from being out of position where they are joined.

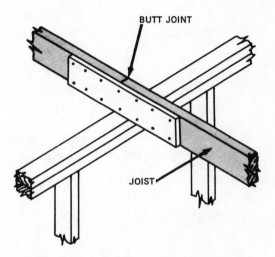

Ceiling joists lapped over the centre support.

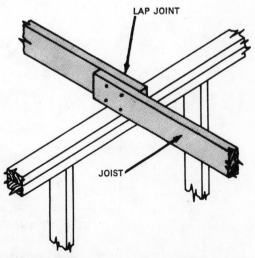

Ceiling joists butted over the centre support.

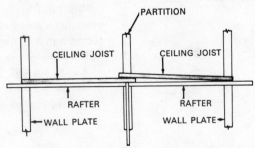

Ceiling joist forced out of position by centre lap.

To frame the ceiling:

When laying out the positions of the ceiling joists and nailing them in place, follow these instructions.

1. The first ceiling joist should be positioned even with the inside edge of the end wall plate. Mark its position on both side wall plates and the supporting partition.

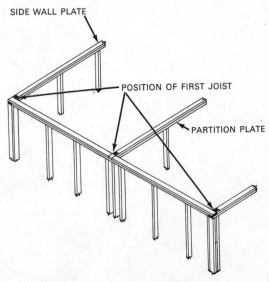

The position of the first ceiling joist.

2. Since plaster lath and several other ceiling coverings come in 1200 mm lengths or widths, it is important that the centre of each joist be positioned every 400 mm along the ceiling. Stretch a steel tape measure from the inside edge of the end wall plate along the side wall plate. Measure 400 mm to the centre of the

first joist and mark the plate. Measure back half the thickness of a joist and square a line across the plate. Mark an "X" beside the line and through the 400 mm mark.

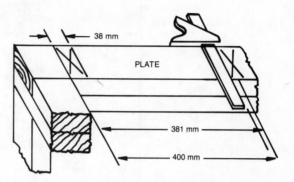

Measuring and marking the first joist positions.

3. Hold the end of a tape measure on this first joist line and mark the plate every 400 mm. Square a line across the plate at each mark and draw an "X" on the same side of each line as you did for the first one.

   This spacing is so commonly used that your tape measure is probably marked every 400 mm.

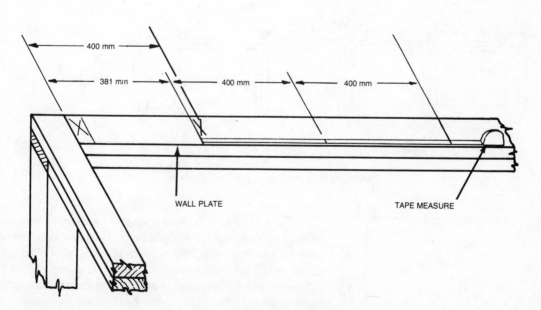

Marking the plate every 400 mm.

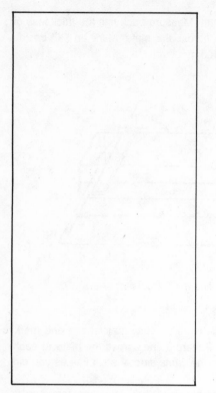

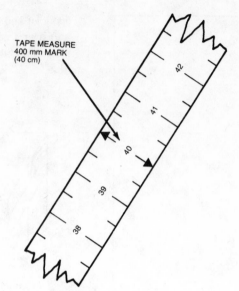

TAPE MEASURE
400 mm MARK
(40 cm)

Some tape measures are marked every 400 mm.

4. Mark the thickness of the joists by tracing a piece of 38 mm scrap. The scrap piece must be placed against the locating line so that it covers the "X."

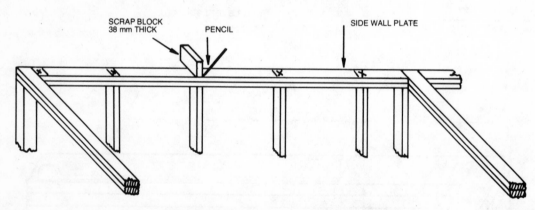

SCRAP BLOCK
38 mm THICK

PENCIL

SIDE WALL PLATE

Marking joist thickness on the top plate.

This is a good time to mark the rafter locations on the ridge board. Lay straight lengths of ridge board material along the wall plate so that their joints will be centred on a rafter. The ridge board should be wide enough to cover the plumb end of the rafters. Allow the ridge board to project past the end walls for the gable overhang. Remember that the rafters will be nailed to the sides of the ceiling joists.

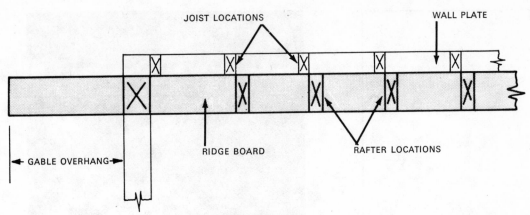

JOIST LOCATIONS

WALL PLATE

GABLE OVERHANG

RIDGE BOARD

RAFTER LOCATIONS

Marking rafter locations on the ridge board.

5. When all of the joist positions have been marked on all of their support plates, measure the distance from the outside of the wall plates to the middle of the support partition. Square the ends and cut the joists to length.

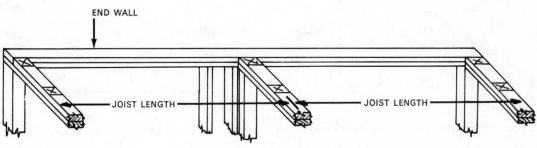

END WALL

JOIST LENGTH

JOIST LENGTH

Determining the length of ceiling joists.

6. Since the rafters and joists will be nailed together, each joist must be cut to match the top edge of the rafter against which it fits.

   In order to do this accurately, lay a rafter on a short piece of joist material as shown, and mark along the rafter with a pencil. When this corner is cut off, the short piece can be used as a pattern to mark all of the joists. Be sure to keep any slight crown of the joists facing upwards.

7. Set the ceiling joists in position on their location marks, and toe-nail them to the plates with 75 mm nails, two on each side of the joist.

The ends of the ceiling joists cut to fit the rafter slope.

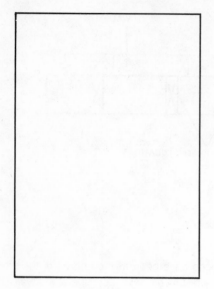

RAFTER

SCRAP PIECE

Making a pattern to mark joist end cuts.

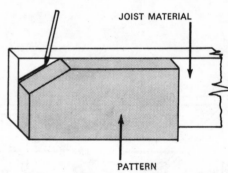

JOIST MATERIAL

PATTERN

Using a pattern to mark the end cuts.

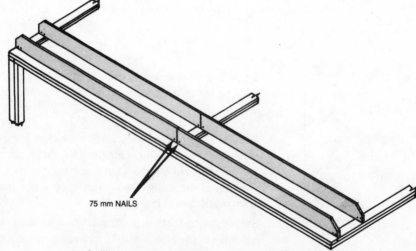

75 mm NAILS

Ceiling joists positioned and nailed to the plates.

8. Cut 1 m lengths of 19 mm lumber and nail them to joists where they butt together. The 19 mm material should be the same width as the joists.

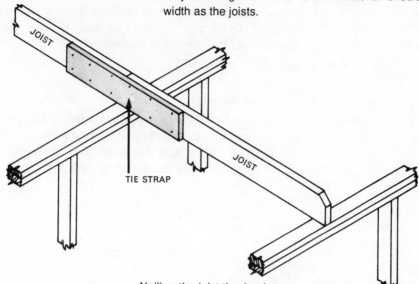

Nailing the joist ties in place.

9. Bridging should be installed between the ceiling joists in the same way as bridging for floor joists. Solid bridging is preferred because it acts as a firestop.

10. When a non-bearing partition runs across a building in the same direction as the ceiling joists, a 19 mm by 140 mm piece is nailed to the top plate to serve as a nailing strip for the inside wall covering. 38 mm by 89 mm bridging between the joists helps hold the nailing strip in place.

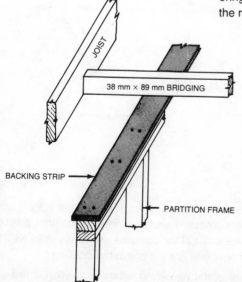

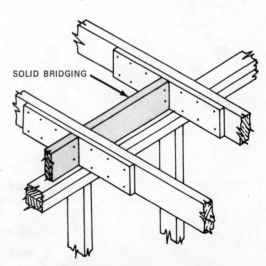

A backing strip installed on a non-bearing partition.

Solid bridging installed as a firestop.

BUILDING THE ROOF

When the ceiling joists are nailed in position, the ridge board is marked and cut, and the rafters are ready to install, the roof may be assembled. The roof in this example will overhang at the gable ends as well as at the eaves.

To raise the roof:

1. Raise the first pair of rafters into position, and place a scrap of ridge board material between their plumb cuts to hold them apart. The seat cuts should fit the wall plate. Drive four 75 mm nails through each rafter and into the ceiling joists.

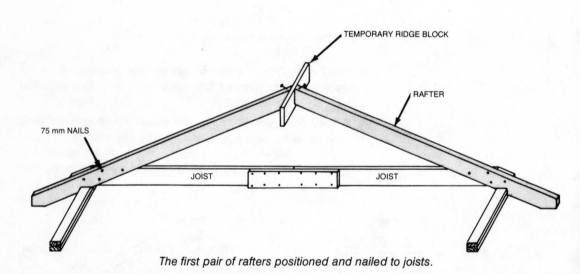

TEMPORARY RIDGE BLOCK

RAFTER

75 mm NAILS

JOIST   JOIST

The first pair of rafters positioned and nailed to joists.

2. Raise pairs of rafters in this way at each joint in the ridge board. Remove the spacer blocks. Raise the ridge board into position and toenail the rafters to it at the positions previously marked. The roof frame should now look like the one in the drawing.

3. Position and nail all of the remaining rafters in position at the wall plates and ridge board.

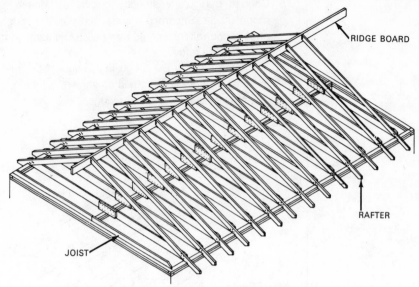

Rafters fastened to the ridge board and joists.

4. Measure from the ridge board along the top edge of each rafter and mark the collar beam location. Hold a length of 38 mm by 89 mm lumber across a pair of rafters at these marks and draw a pencil along it, even with the top edges of the rafters. Cut the 38 mm by 89 mm piece to shape. Use it as a pattern to cut a collar beam for each pair of rafters; use 75 mm nails to fasten the collar beams in place.

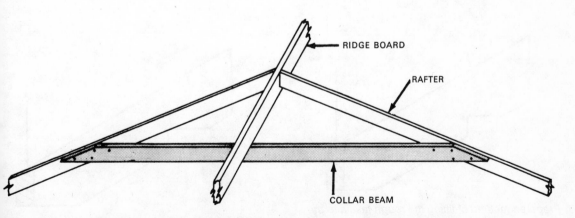

A collar beam installed across two rafters increases their strength.

5. Choose particularly straight lengths of 38 mm lumber for the rough fascia. Square the ends and nail the rough fascia to the ends of the rafters with 90 mm nails. Any joints in the fascia must be made at a rafter.

   The top edge of the rough fascia should be made using either the prepared or fitted method as shown. A hand plane or a power saw may be used to bevel the edge.

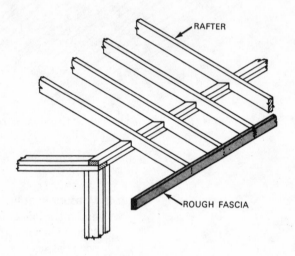

The rough fascia should be extended for the gable overhang.

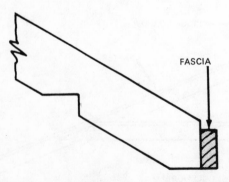

Prepared method of fitting the rough fascia to the rafters.

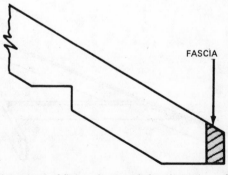

Fitted method of fitting the rough fascia to the rafter.

Before the roof construction can be completed, the gable ends must be built to support the roof overhang. Roofs that do not have an overhang at the gables use pairs of rafters positioned even with the end walls. Upright studs are cut and positioned to frame the gable ends.

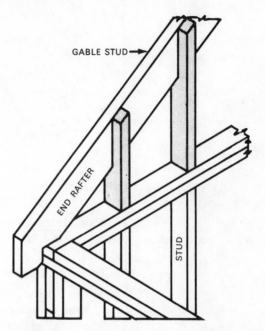

Framing a gable for a roof with no overhang.

Roofs that do not have an overhang are not very attractive and do not provide weather protection for walls, windows and doors.

In most areas of the country, gable overhangs of no more than 300 mm may be built onto the gable. Greater overhangs require more support than this method allows.

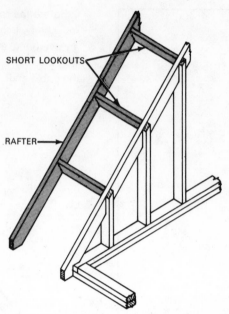

Lookout rafters are nailed to the gable rafters if the overhang is slight

To frame a gable and roof overhang:

1. Use a pencil and one of the scrap pieces cut from the top end of a rafter to mark the ridge board. The top plate of the gable end will be fitted against this mark.

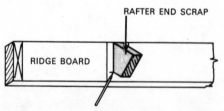

Marking the position of the gable plate on the ridge board.

2. Four rafters should have been cut for the ends of the roof overhang. Use one of these to mark the length and cuts of the gable top plate on a length of 38 mm by 89 mm lumber.

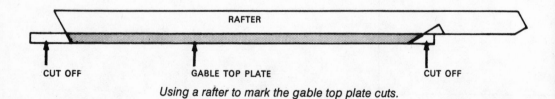

Using a rafter to mark the gable top plate cuts.

3. Mark and cut two of these pieces for each gable, and nail them to the ridge board and wall plate.

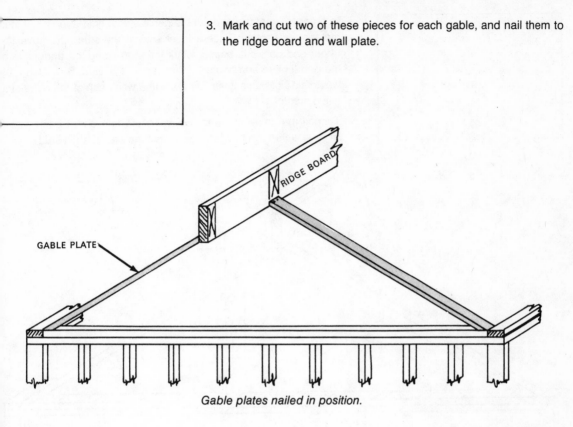

Gable plates nailed in position.

4. The gable studs should be positioned directly over the full-length studs in the end walls. Mark the wall plates as shown in the drawing.

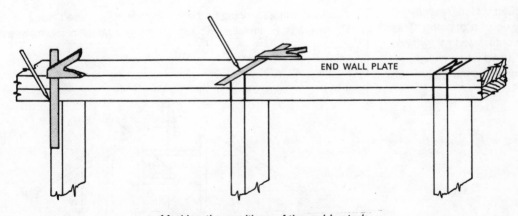

Marking the positions of the gable studs

5. In order to measure and cut the gable studs, hold a length of stud material as shown. Place a level against the stud and move the upper end until it is plumb. Mark the stud along the underside of the gable plate and square a line across the stud. Saw along the waste side of these lines. Do the same with each of the remaining gable studs.

6. Toenail the gable studs to the wall plate and check each with a level. Nail through the gable plate into the end of each stud.

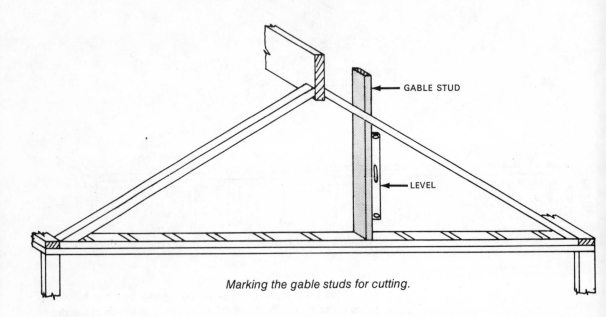

GABLE STUD

LEVEL

Marking the gable studs for cutting.

ventilator: An opening through which fresh air may enter a building. This prevents wood rot, which is caused when moisture builds up in the attic.

7. Usually, a screened **ventilator** is installed on both gable ends as close to the ridge of the roof as possible. The drawing shows the rough frame opening for such a ventilator. Screened metal ventilators must be installed in such roof styles as the hip and mansard.

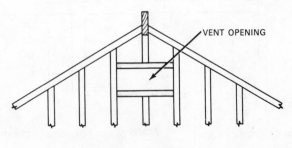

VENT OPENING

A framed opening for an attic vent.

Some of the lookout rafters in place.

BUILDING THE GABLE OVERHANG

The framework that forms a gable overhang is sometimes called a **ladder** because of its appearance. The rungs of the ladder are called the **lookout rafters**. These lookouts must be positioned carefully, especially when plywood will be used to sheath the roof or the underside of the overhang, in order to support the edges of the sheets.

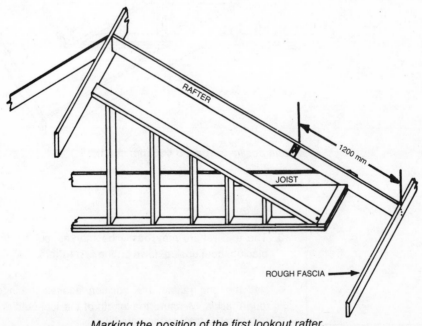

Marking the position of the first lookout rafter.

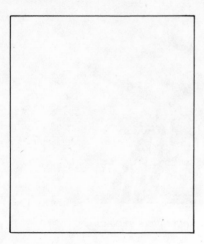

How to build the gable overhang:

1. To mark the position of the first lookout on each side of the gables, measure 1200 mm from the outside edge of the rough fascia along the first rafter. Use a square to mark the position of the lookout as shown. Note that the 1200 mm mark is the centre of the lookout rafter.

2. Measure from one side of this first lookout position along the rafter, and mark lookout positions every 400 mm. Square a line across the rafter at each of these points, and mark the lookout positions with an "X."

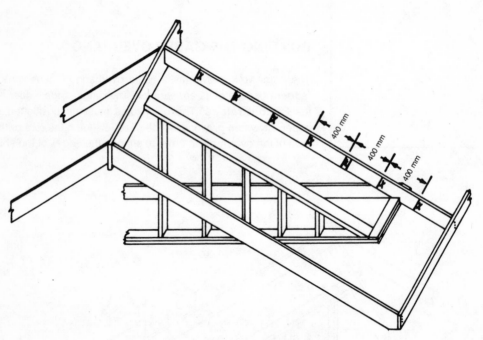

Lookout positions spaced 400 mm apart.

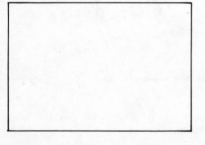

3. The end rafters may easily be marked out for the lookouts by placing them upside down on the first rafters.

4. Nail the end rafters into position against the ridge board and rough fascia. Measure the length of the lookouts and cut the correct number from rafter material.

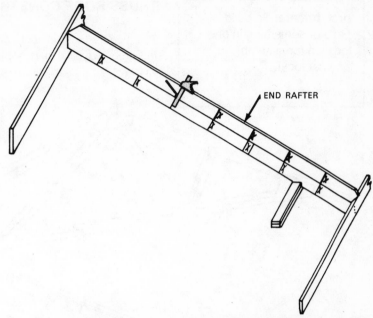

END RAFTER

Marking the lookout positions on the end rafters.

5. Nail the lookouts in place with 90 mm nails driven through the rafters into the lookouts. Toenail each lookout to the gable plate with 60 mm nails. The drawing shows the completed overhang on one side of the gable.

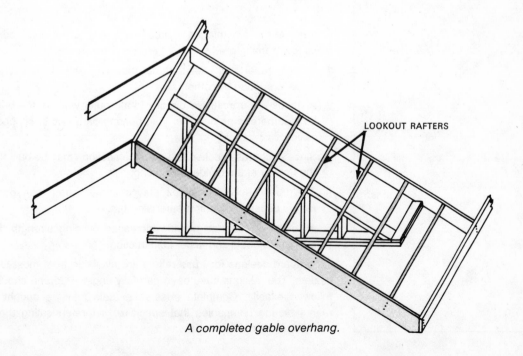

LOOKOUT RAFTERS

A completed gable overhang.

TRUSS ROOF CONSTRUCTION

> **prefabricate:** To build parts of something in one location for assembly in another location.

The modern trend in roof construction is toward the **prefabricated** truss roof. A typical truss section is shown here.

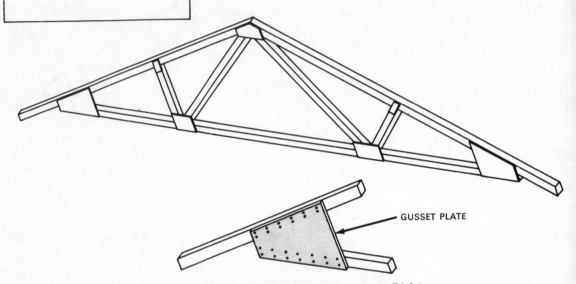

GUSSET PLATE

A truss roof section with plywood gussets at all joints.

Some of the advantages of truss roof construction over conven-tional roof framing are:

1. Smaller rafter and joist material may be used since each part helps to support the others.

2. All loads are transferred directly to the outer walls of the building so that there is no need for load bearing partitions to support the ceiling.

3. Since each truss section is a unit, the sections may be built flat on the floor or at the builder's workshop.

4. The truss sections may be placed farther apart than ordinary rafters because of their greater strength.

5. All of these features provide increased building strength, lower cost of materials and faster construction.

Standard designs for truss rafters are available from most lumber dealers. The designs have been carefully engineered and should be followed exactly. Complete truss rafter sets may be bought from manufacturing companies that specialize in prefabricating them in many sizes and shapes.

POST-AND-BEAM ROOF CONSTRUCTION

When a roof is built with a post-and-beam frame, the size of each framing member is much larger than in more conventional frames but there are fewer of them. As the drawing shows, the ridge board becomes a ridge beam and the rafters are heavy and widely spaced. 38 mm or 64 mm thick tongue-and-groove planks form the roof sheathing.

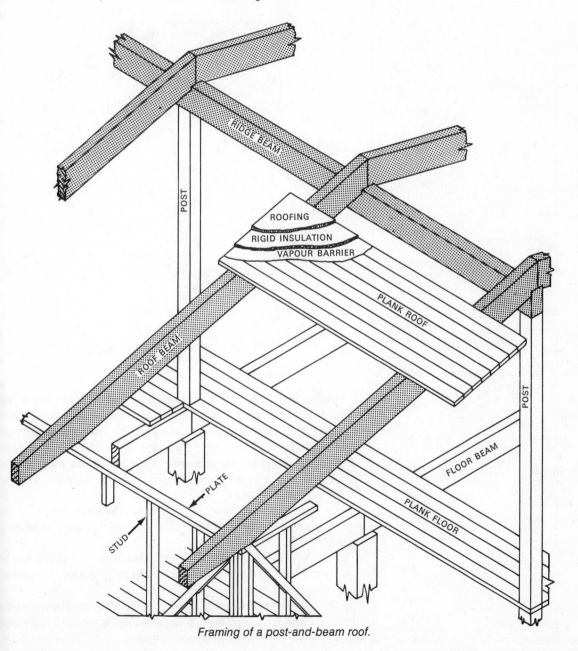

Framing of a post-and-beam roof.

Wide roofs need lengthwise beams in addition to the ridge beam. In some cases, no heavy rafters are used at all. To make sure that heavy roof loads do not cause heavy beams to shift apart, one of the methods pictured should be used to fasten them in place.

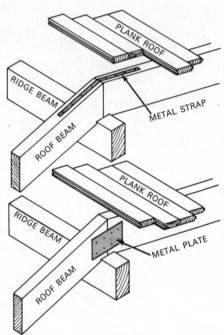

Two methods of fastening roof beams together.

timber: A large squared or planed length of lumber.

The beams need not be solid **timbers**. In fact, in most parts of the country it would be difficult to find straight, solid timbers in the sizes and lengths needed for this job. To have the beams shipped from distant sources would add greatly to the cost of the already expensive wood. Therefore, the glue-laminated beam and the plywood box beam are widely used. Rafter beams made of standard sizes of lumber are also shown.

The glue-laminated beam is a manufactured beam that must be put together and glued in a large press. Beams of many shapes may be formed.

The plywood box beam may be assembled at the building site in any required length. Its strength is equal to or greater than other beam types at a much lower cost.

The post-and-beam roof is usually so attractive on the underside that no joists or ceilings need be installed in the rooms. The beams and roof sheathing are finished with varnish.

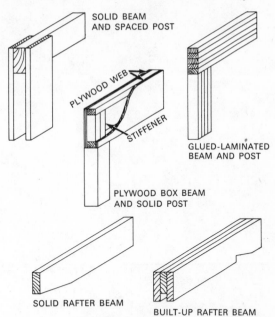

SOLID BEAM
AND SPACED POST

PLYWOOD WEB

STIFFENER

GLUED-LAMINATED
BEAM AND POST

PLYWOOD BOX BEAM
AND SOLID POST

SOLID RAFTER BEAM

BUILT-UP RAFTER BEAM

Styles of main and rafter beams used in post-and-beam roofs.

An exposed beamed ceiling.

CHAPTER 9

Sheathing

WATCH FOR THESE WORDS

fiberboard   lath
gypsum

HOW TO USE THESE WORDS

1. **Fiberboard** is made of small wood fibres pressed into flat sheets.
2. **Gypsum** is a type of powdered rock used to make drywall panels.
3. Small sheets of gypsum board **lath** may be nailed to the wall and ceiling frames to act as a base for wet plaster.

FIND THE ANSWERS TO THESE QUESTIONS

1. List two sheathing materials used under wood lap siding.
2. List two sheathing materials used under brick veneer wall coverings.
3. What advantages are there to installing lumber sheathing diagonally rather than horizontally?
4. Describe the correct method for positioning the first diagonal sheathing board.
5. List two advantages of plywood sheathing over lumber sheathing.
6. In which direction should the face grain of plywood sheathing be installed on a wall frame?
7. How does tongue-and-groove edged plywood save time during installation?
8. How far apart should the nails be spaced to fasten plywood sheathing to the wall studs?

9. Why are let-in or cut-in frame braces needed when using fiberboard sheets or gypsum board for sheathing?

10. Should fiberboard sheets be installed vertically or horizontally? Why?

11. How is fiberboard installed around window and door openings?

12. What type of nails should be used to fasten fiberboard and gypsum board to the wall frame?

The first covering over the wall and roof framing is called sheathing. When choosing the sheathing material you should consider the style of frame, the type of finishing material that will be applied over the sheathing, and whether additional bracing and heat insulation are needed.

WALL SHEATHING

When finish siding materials such as wood lap siding or shingles are used, they must be nailed to the sheathing. Therefore, the sheathing must be made of either plywood or lumber. Fiberboard or gypsum board may be used as sheathing material when the finish siding needs to be fastened only to the wall studs. Brick veneer wall covering is an example of this kind of finish siding.

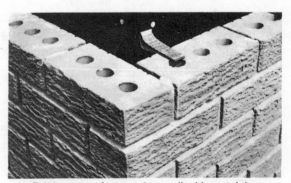

Brick veneer fastened to wall with metal ties.

All types of wall sheathing should cover the whole wooden framework from the bottom edge of the sole to the top edge of the top plate to give the framework maximum strength and make it airtight.

Lumber sheathing is usually applied diagonally so that extra frame bracing is not needed.

A building would be weak if lumber sheathing were applied horizontally.

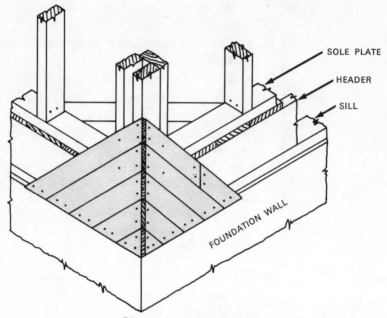

SOLE PLATE

HEADER

SILL

FOUNDATION WALL

Diagonal wood sheathing.

The boards used for sheathing should be 19 mm thick ship-lap or tongue-and-groove lumber. Use two or three 65 mm nails at each stud to fasten the sheathing boards to the frame. All joints in the sheathing should centre on a stud so that both ends of the joint can be nailed to the stud.

A combination square may be used to mark the 45° cuts on the ends of diagonal sheathing boards.

Horizontal wood sheathing.

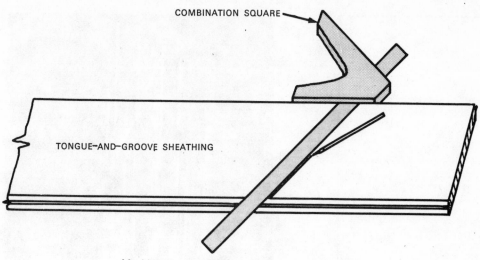

Marking the end cuts on diagonal sheathing.

The position of the first board may be marked out by measuring equal distances from the corner of the sill plate, along the sill and up the corner post.

Allow the ends of the sheathing boards to extend past the corners until they are nailed in place, then saw them off one or two at a time. When applying sheathing around door or window openings, the ends are cut even with the inside edge of the opening.

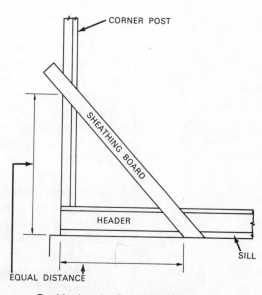

Positioning the first sheathing board.

Sheathing around a door opening.

The strongest wall is probably made when plywood panels 12.5 mm or 9.5 mm thick are used as wall sheathing. Since each sheet covers a large area, the walls are sheathed in a fraction of the time it takes to apply board sheathing. The face grain of plywood panels should be laid crosswise to the wall studs to give maximum strength and to avoid bowing between the studs. Fasten the plywood with 45 mm nails spaced 150 mm apart along the panel edges, and 300 mm apart along the inside parts of the panel. A 2400 mm wall height can be covered with two widths of plywood. The ends of the panels must be staggered so that they do not meet on the same wall stud. The sill and header are sheathed with a strip of plywood sawed to the correct width.

The practice of sheathing the sill and header separately has become fairly standard because it allows for possible differences in shrinkage of the wall frame and floor frame.

When square-edged panels are used, their edges must be supported between the studs by 38 mm by 89 mm bridging. Tongue-and-groove panels do not need this edge support.

Fiberboard sheathing has no grain and therefore may be applied either horizontally or vertically. Its strength will not be affected. However, the sheets are usually installed vertically to avoid the problem of

fiberboard: A flat sheet material made of pressed wood fibres.

edge support between the studs. Sheets of 1200 mm by 2745 mm fiberboard installed vertically will usually cover the entire height of the framework.

Since this material is not expensive, the sheets are laid over the entire wall, covering the window openings and sometimes the door openings. The fiberboard over the openings is then cut out with a hand saw.

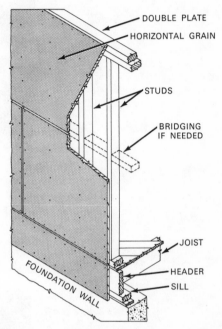

The correct way to install plywood sheathing.

Fiberboard sheathing on a wall.

gypsum: Finely ground limestone.

lath: Wood strips or small sheets of gypsum board used as a base for wet plaster.

Gypsum board sheathing is similar to plaster **lath** and gypsum wallboard material. It has a gypsum core covered on both sides and on the edges with paper. The paper is treated to resist water.

Both gypsum board and fiberboard must be nailed every 75 mm along the edges and every 200 mm on inner studs. Use special broad headed nails 45 mm long. Install the end joints so that they are not located one above the other on the same stud.

Gypsum board panels.

Gypsum board sheathing installation.

ROOF SHEATHING

WATCH FOR THESE WORDS

run   spline
rabbet   soffit

HOW TO USE THESE WORDS

1. Sometimes sheathing boards tend to **run** crookedly across a roof frame.
2. Ship-lap lumber is **rabbeted** so that its edges overlap.
3. Grooved lumber may be joined with a thin strip of wood called a **spline**.
4. The underside of a roof overhang is called the **soffit**.

FIND THE ANSWERS TO THESE QUESTIONS

1. Describe two types of lumber roof sheathing.
2. What precaution should be taken to keep the sheathing boards from running crookedly?
3. How does the use of plywood sheathing reduce the cost of a large roof?
4. Describe three methods of supporting plywood edges between the rafters.
5. Why should a space be left between the plywood sheets?
6. Why must special care be taken when installing plank sheathing on a beam roof?
7. Why is such heavy sheathing needed on a post-and-beam frame?
8. What materials are commonly used to cover the roof soffits?
9. How does the amount of roof overhang affect the style of soffit construction used?

Sheathing a roof is much like sheathing a wall. However, the material used must provide a nailing surface for shingles. Either 19 mm thick tongue-and-groove or ship-lap lumber, or 7.5 to 12.5 mm thick sheathing-grade plywood, is used to sheath conventional roofs. Tongue-and-groove planks 38 to 64 mm thick are used for post-and-beam roofs.

To install lumber sheathing:

1. Square one end of a straight length of sheathing lumber, and install it even with the edge of the rough fascia as shown.

The squared end should be centred on the top edge of a rafter and the other end should be even with the outer edge of the gable rafter or extend past it. Any slight overhang may be sawed off later.

2. Continue to apply sheathing along the edge of the roof until it is complete from one end to the other. The ends of each board must be nailed to a rafter. Saw off any excess length so that the sheathing is even with the gable rafter.

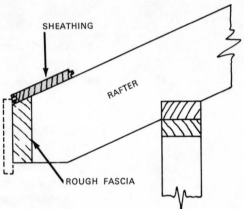

Tongue-and-groove sheathing installed even with the fascia.

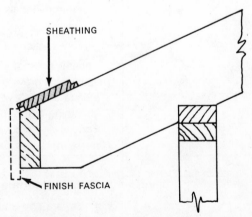

Rabbet-edged sheathing installed even with rough fascia.

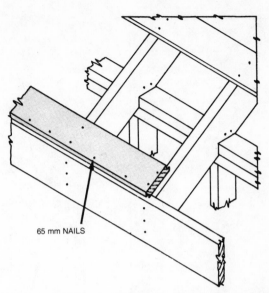

65 mm NAILS

Joints in sheathing must meet in the middle of a rafter.

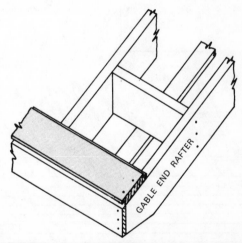

GABLE END RAFTER

Saw the ends of sheathing even with the gable end rafter.

3. Fit the next run of sheathing tightly against the first, and continue up the roof to the ridge. The end joints should not come together on the same rafter.

It is wise to check the distance across the sheathing at the ends and middle of the roof from time to time in order to avoid a gradual **run** of the sheathing. A board that is too narrow at one end or fits poorly will cause the sheathing to run at an angle or on a curve across the rafters.

run: This word as used here means that sheathing boards have not been fastened parallel to each other.

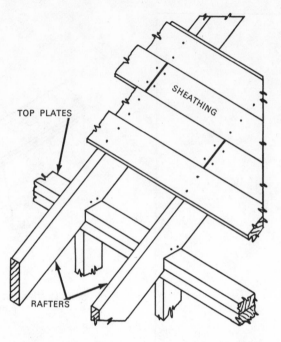

Joints in the sheathing runs should not come together on the same rafter.

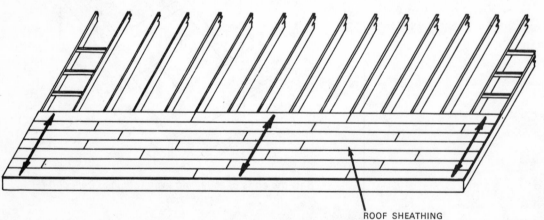

Measure the sheathing at these points to make sure it is straight.

4. Both sides of the roof should be completed up to the ridge, and the last sheathing boards should be cut and fitted at the ridge as shown.

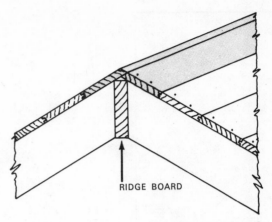

RIDGE BOARD

The sheathing must be cut and fitted at the ridge.

PLYWOOD SHEATHING

Large roofs may be covered in much less time if plywood is used for sheathing. Since labour costs are high, the length of time taken to build a house is very important.

The minimum thickness of plywood used depends on the rafter spacing. Rafters spaced 300 mm apart may be sheathed with 7.5 mm plywood. 9.5 mm plywood is used with 400 mm rafter spacing, and 12.5 mm plywood for spacings of 600 mm. If the panel edges are supported by blocking or metal clips, or if the edges are tongue-and-groove, the next thinner size of plywood may be used.

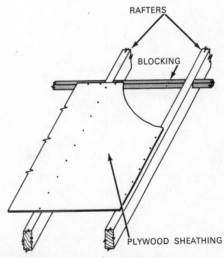

RAFTERS

BLOCKING

PLYWOOD SHEATHING

Blocking used to support edges of plywood sheathing.

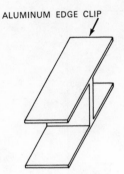

ALUMINUM EDGE CLIP

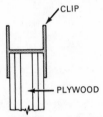

CLIP

PLYWOOD

Metal clips are used to support the edges of plywood sheathing between the rafters.

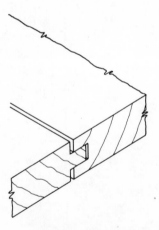

TONGUE-AND-GROOVE
EDGE MATCH

Tongue-and-groove plywood needs no extra support.

The surface grain of the plywood sheets should be installed cross-wise to the rafters. A loose fit between the sheets is best to allow for expansion in damp weather.

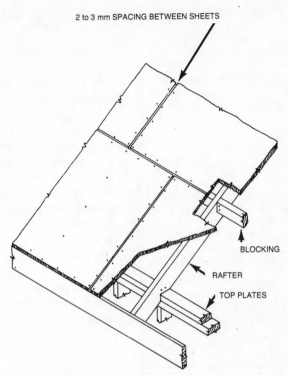

2 to 3 mm SPACING BETWEEN SHEETS

BLOCKING

RAFTER

TOP PLATES

Space the plywood sheets and alternate their end joints.

Install the first row of panels even with the edge of the rough fascia. The finish fascia will cover the edge of the sheathing. Use 50 mm nails 150 mm apart along the panel edges and 300 mm apart in the centre areas.

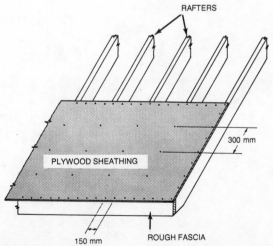

RAFTERS

300 mm

PLYWOOD SHEATHING

150 mm

ROUGH FASCIA

The plywood should be positioned even with the fascia.

PLANK SHEATHING

The extra thickness of sheathing for post-and-beam roofs is needed to span the large distances between roof beams. The drawings show some of the ways in which planks are fitted for greater strength and an attractive appearance.

The installation of plank sheathing is much the same as when 19 mm lumber is used, with a few differences. Since in many cases the underside of the planks will be the finish ceiling, this surface must be freshly planed, and care must be taken to prevent it from becoming marked or dirty.

Post-and-beam roofs are noted for their very large overhangs at the eaves and gables. Very often there is no support for the planks along these roof edges; the ends of the roof beams may remain visible.

The nails used to fasten the planks to the roof beams will be 100 mm long for 38 mm planks and 300 mm long for 64 mm planks. A heavy hammer makes this nailing job much faster and easier. End joints should be centred on the roof beams unless the ends of the planks are tongue-and-groove matched.

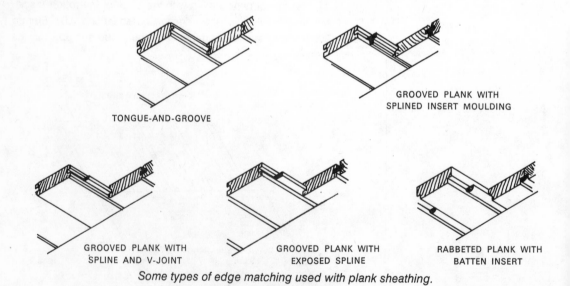

TONGUE-AND-GROOVE

GROOVED PLANK WITH
SPLINED INSERT MOULDING

GROOVED PLANK WITH
SPLINE AND V-JOINT

GROOVED PLANK WITH
EXPOSED SPLINE

RABBETED PLANK WITH
BATTEN INSERT

Some types of edge matching used with plank sheathing.

rabbet: A wide plow cut along the edge of a length of lumber.

spline: A thin strip of wood made to fit and join the edges of grooved lumber.

soffit: The underside of any roof overhang.

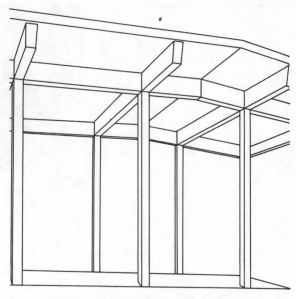

A typical post-and-beam roof overhang.

SOFFIT FRAMING

The underside of the roof overhang is usually covered for a finer appearance and greater ease in painting. This **soffit** area may be covered with narrow matched lumber or plywood nailed directly to the rafters and rough fascia. The photographs show the framing and finishing of a level soffit.

Often the amount of roof overhang determines the style of soffit construction used. Two methods are shown.

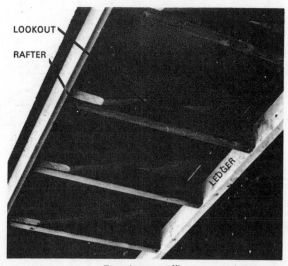

Framing a soffit.

A completed soffit at the gable end.

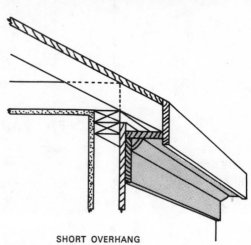

SHORT OVERHANG

One soffit finishing method.

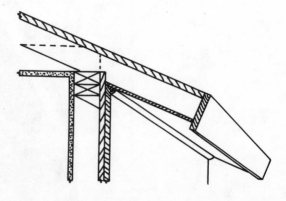

SLOPING SOFFIT

Another method of soffit finishing.

CHAPTER 10

Shingling

WATCH FOR THESE WORDS

flashing
galvanized
felt
asphalt
mineral

tabs
eaves
solder
flux

HOW TO USE THESE WORDS

1. Metal **flashing** may be made of **galvanized** steel.
2. Roll roofing is made of heavy **felt** that has been soaked with **asphalt** and coated with small **mineral** particles.
3. Asphalt shingles may have one, two, or three **tabs**.
4. Shingles should be supported by a metal flashing along the **eaves**.
5. A **flux** is needed to **solder** copper or galvanized steel.

FIND THE ANSWERS TO THESE QUESTIONS

1. What kind of wood is commonly used for wood shingles?
2. How many bundles of shingles are needed to cover both sides of a roof that measures 3 m by 7 m on each side?
3. Why should a strip of wood be nailed temporarily to the rough fascia?
4. What material is used to make flashing for roof valleys?
5. Why is it necessary to apply a double thickness of shingles along the edge of the roof?

6. How can you make certain that the shingle courses are running even with the ridge?

7. Why is the first course of asphalt three-in-one shingles applied with the tabs facing up the roof?

8. Why must half of the first tab be cut off when starting the second course of three-in-one shingles?

9. What determines whether roll roofing must be used instead of shingles?

10. Why is fine white gravel sprinkled on a built-up roll roof?

11. What is the purpose of metal flashing around a chimney?

12. Why must the flashing be installed during the shingling operation?

As soon as possible after the roof sheathing is completed, the roof should be made weathertight. Roofs that have a pitch of 1 to 6 or greater may be covered with shingles. Roll roofing is recommended for roofs with a lower pitch. There are many types, styles and colours of roofing materials for both types of roof.

All types of roofing material must be fastened securely to the roof. It is very important that you use the correct procedure so that the roof will withstand years of wind, rain and snow. This chapter describes the application of some of the more common roof coverings in use.

WOOD SHINGLES

Wood shingles are probably the oldest type of roof covering still in use, and are still considered by many people to be the most attractive. These shingles are usually made of cedar which has a natural resistance to weather. If a coat of roof preservative stain is applied every four or five years, wood shingles will outlast many of the more modern roof coverings. Preservative stains are available in many attractive colours.

Cedar shingles vary greatly in width but they are always 400 mm, 450 mm, or 600 mm in length. They are sold in bundles.

One bundle of 400 mm shingles holds enough to cover 2.63 m^2 of roof area so that 140 mm of shingle is showing.

Example

The gable roof shown in the drawing has a length of 8000 mm (8 m) and a width of 4000 mm (4 m).

Area on each side:

$8 \times 4 = 32$ m^2

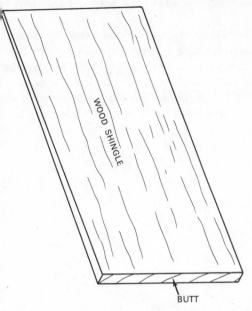

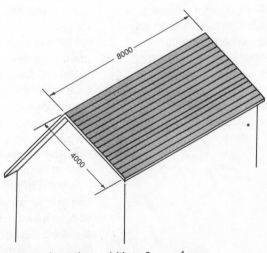

Wood shingles.

Total area:

$32 \times 2 = 64 \text{ m}^2$

Number of bundles of 400 mm shingles needed to cover the roof:

$\dfrac{64}{2.63} = 24.33$

Of course, you would buy 25 bundles.

Length $\times$ width $\times$ 2 = roof area.

The pitch of the roof should be at least 1 to 4 when wood shingles a[...] used.

Before beginning any shingling job, you should sweep the sheathi[...] clean with a broom and check the entire roof to make sure the naili[...] of the sheathing is complete. To make sure that the shingles har[...] over the finish fascia, either install it at this time, or nail a rough strip [...] 19 mm by 38 mm lumber in its place. This strip will be removed aft[...] the shingling has been completed so that the finish fascia can be i[...] stalled free of ladder marks.

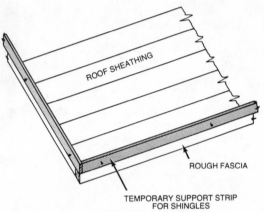

A temporary support for the shingle edges.

flashing: A piece of sheet metal, either copper or galvanized steel. It is bent to fit along roof valleys, around chimneys or in any place where there is danger of leakage from rain or melting snow.

galvanized: Plated with zinc to prevent rust.

If the roof you are shingling has another roof adjoining it, a **met[...] flashing** must be installed in the valleys before shingling begins. Th[...] flashing is usually made of **galvanized** iron that has been folded [...] form a ridge down the centre of the valley. The ridge prevents ra[...] water from rushing down one roof and under the shingles of the othe[...] roof.

Flashing material is referred to by several names: galvanized iro[...] galvanized steel or sheet metal. Any of these materials may be use[...]

Make certain the roof sheathing is dry. Try to choose a period of d[...] weather for the shingling operation. Carry enough bundles of shingle[...] to the roof to last several hours so that you will not be walking on th[...] shingled section any more than is necessary. Set the bundles down [...] various locations on the roof. Open only one bundle for each perso[...] shingling to reduce the number of loose shingles that the wind ca[...] blow off the roof.

In order to prevent yourself from slipping off the roof, you shoul[...] wear rubber soled shoes. If the roof is steep, you should build a sma[...] shingler's seat to fit the slope of the roof. Two nails hammered into th[...] sheathing will hold the seat in place. Wear a carpenter's apron with [...] good supply of shingle nails in the pockets.

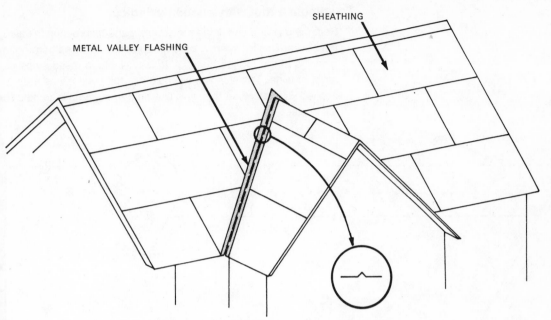

The joint between two roofs must be flashed.

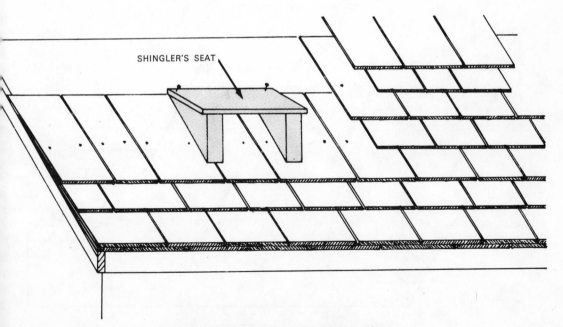

A simple shingler's seat for steep roofs.

To shingle a roof with wooden shingles:

1. Beginning at one end of the roof, apply a sheet of roofing felt along the eaves. This felt improves the windproofing and weatherproofing qualities of the roofing material. It is available in rolled strips that are 1 m wide. The shingles will hold this felt securely as they are applied. Therefore, at this time use only enough nails to hold the felt in place.

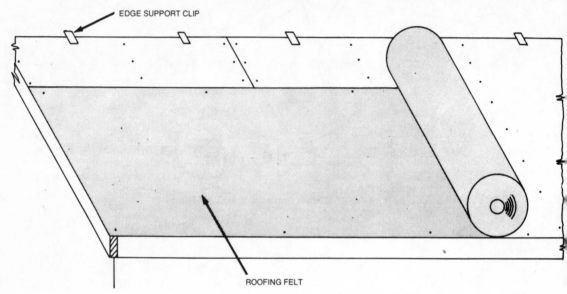

EDGE SUPPORT CLIP

ROOFING FELT

Roofing felt applied under the shingles.

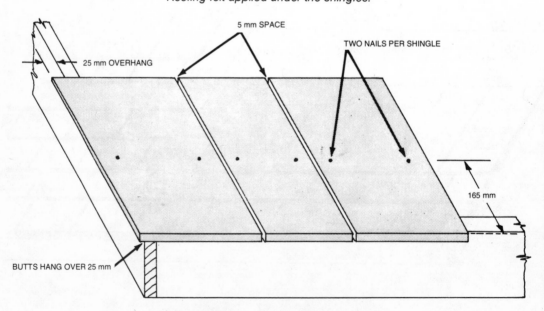

5 mm SPACE

TWO NAILS PER SHINGLE

25 mm OVERHANG

165 mm

BUTTS HANG OVER 25 mm

Nailing the first row of wood shingles in place.

2. Nail the first row of shingles in place along the eaves, allowing 25 mm to hang over the rough support strip. Use only two nails per shingle. Space the shingles 5 mm apart to give them room to swell when wet.

3. The sheathing has not yet been covered between the shingles. A second course of shingles must be laid over the first course to cover the joints by at least 40 mm.

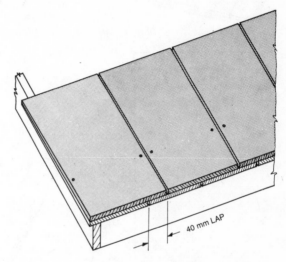

The second course of shingles covers the first.

4. Measure 140 mm up from the bottom of the double row of shingles and nail a shingle in place at both ends of the roof. Stretch a chalk line between these two shingles as shown and snap the line to mark the position of the **shingle butts** (the thick end of the shingle) in this course.

5. Complete this course of shingles by positioning each shingle flush with the chalk line. The joints in the previous course must be over-lapped by at least 40 mm. Be careful not to bruise the shingles with the hammer. The head of each nail should be driven so that it just touches the surface of the shingle but does not sink in.

6. Before the first strip of No. 15 roofing felt is covered, nail the next strip in place with 50 mm overlapping the first strip. Note that if roof-ing felt is not being used and the sheathing is board or plank, it is not necessary to use a chalk line. Position the tops of the shingles parallel with the sheathing joints.

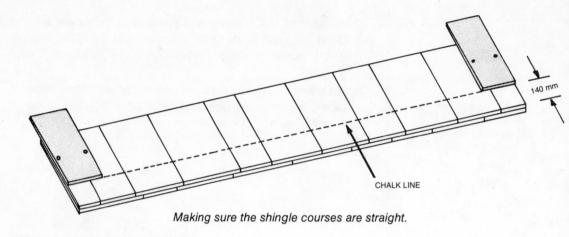

CHALK LINE

Making sure the shingle courses are straight.

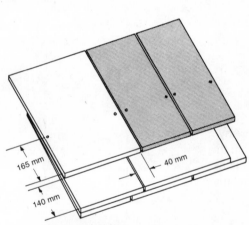

165 mm

40 mm

140 mm

Minimum shingle overlap is 40 mm.

7. Mark and nail each course of shingles in the same way to abou
1 m from the ridge of the roof. At this point, measure down fro
both ends and the middle of the ridge to the shingle course jus
completed. The measurements should all be the same. If they ar
not, the difference must be corrected before the last course
nailed along the ridge. For instance, a 50 mm difference would eas
ily show at the ridge. To correct this error, adjust the chalk lin
10 mm in each of the next five courses. The top ends of the last tw
courses must be sawed off flush with the ridge.

8. When both sides of the roof are completely shingled to the ridge,
ridge cap must be installed. This cap may be made of shingles
lengths of 19 mm lumber, 89 to 140 mm wide. The butt ends of
shingle ridge cap should face away from the prevailing wind, an
the pairs of shingles should overlap with alternate joints.

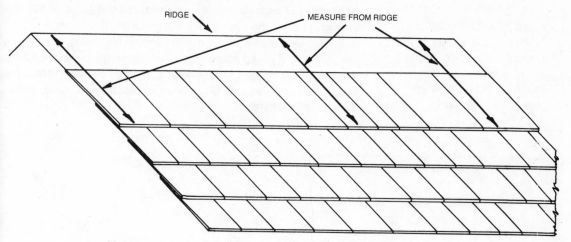

RIDGE   MEASURE FROM RIDGE

Making certain the shingle courses have not become high at one end.

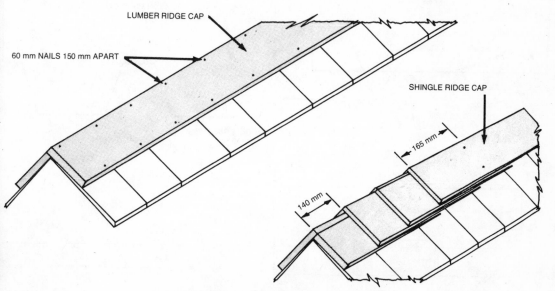

LUMBER RIDGE CAP

60 mm NAILS 150 mm APART

SHINGLE RIDGE CAP

165 mm

140 mm

Two styles of ridge caps used with wood shingles.

ASPHALT SHINGLES

felt: A cloth made of wood and fur.

Asphalt shingles are made of heavy paper **felt** that has been soaked with asphalt and coated with small manufactured granules. The shingles are available in a wide assortment of patterns and colours.

The three-in-one strip shingle, either plain or self sealing, is by far the most popular style of shingle used on modern roofs. Although

asphalt: A dark solid or thick tar-like material found in natural deposits. Asphalt can also be made from materials left over when coal or oil is refined.

other styles of **asphalt** shingles are used, this text will deal only with the installation of the three-in-one shingle strip.

The drawing shows two common patterns for nailing three-in-one shingles. When nailed properly, the nail heads will be covered by at least 25 mm of the next shingle course. The roof sheathing should be swept clean and a strip of rolled roofing felt tack nailed in place, as was done for wood shingles.

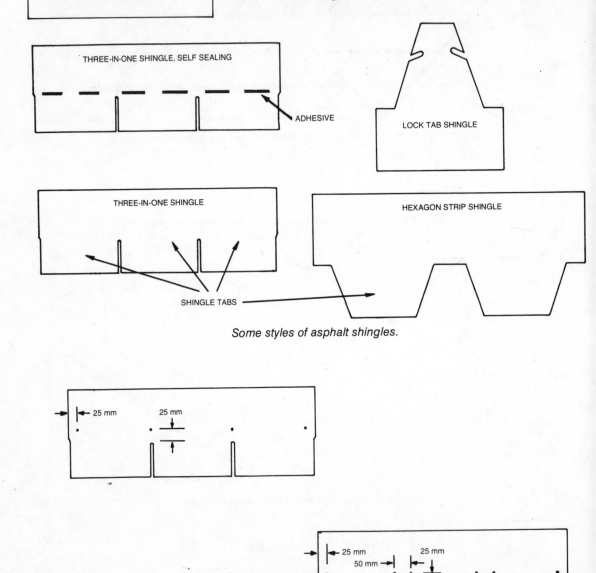

Some styles of asphalt shingles.

Nailing patterns for three-in-one asphalt shingles.

mineral: Any material mined from the earth; a solid that is neither plant nor animal matter.

Roofs that have valley joints are often completely covered along the valleys with roofing felt before the flashing is installed. The flashing may be made of sheet metal as described earlier in this chapter, or it may be built up of **mineral** surfaced roll roofing nailed and cemented in place. In both cases, the shingles are cemented to the flashing with a plastic cement.

Galvanized steel flashing should be nailed along the eaves to support the ends of the shingle tabs and to act as a drip moulding.

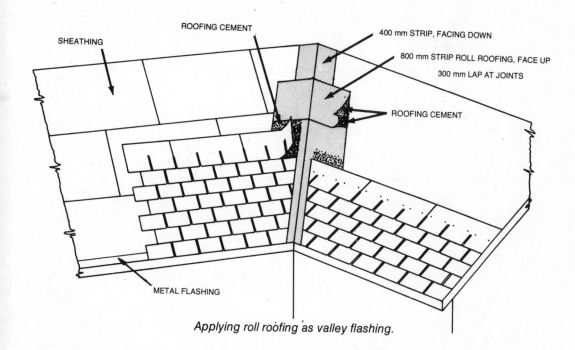

Applying roll roofing as valley flashing.

To shingle a roof with asphalt shingles:

1. Carry enough bundles of shingles to the roof for several hours' work. Open one bundle for each person shingling. Nail a course of shingles in place with the tabs facing up the roof slope or apply a strip of roll roofing. The lower edge of each shingle or the roll roofing should be even with the metal flashing.

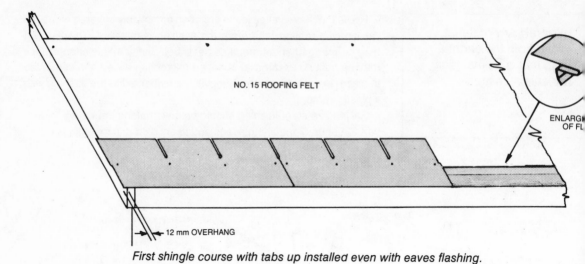

NO. 15 ROOFING FELT

ENLARG
OF FL

←→ 12 mm OVERHANG

First shingle course with tabs up installed even with eaves flashing.

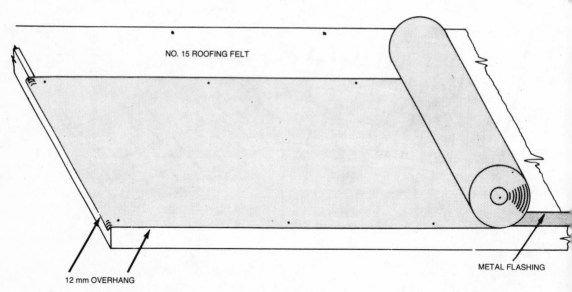

NO. 15 ROOFING FELT

METAL FLASHING

12 mm OVERHANG

Asphalt roll roofing being applied along the roof edge even with the flashing.

tabs: Flaps projecting from a strip of shingle material to look like separate shingles.

2. Nail a course of shingles with the ends of the **tabs** even with th starter strip.

3. The first shingle in the second course must be shortened by half o the first tab so that the joints will not come one above the other. Na the shingles so that the edges of the tabs are even with the ends o the slots in the previous course.

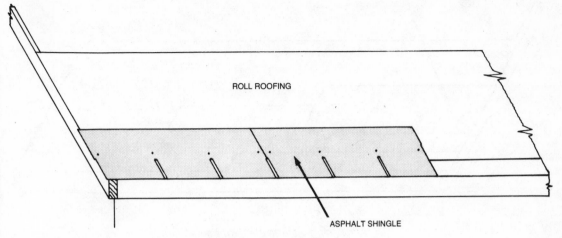

ROLL ROOFING

ASPHALT SHINGLE

The first course of shingles.

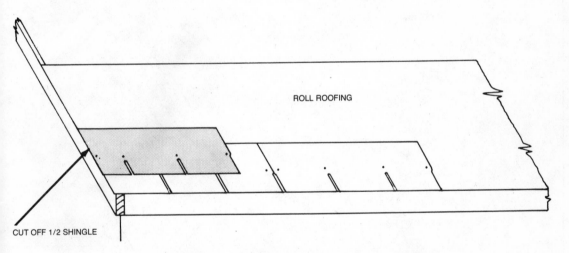

ROLL ROOFING

CUT OFF 1/2 SHINGLE

The first shingle in the second course loses half of the first tab.

eaves: The overhanging lower edge of a roof.

4. The first shingle in the next or third course is a full shingle. The fourth course is like the second, the fifth course starts with a full shingle, and so on up the roof. Measure up from the **eaves** every five or six shingle courses and in several locations along the roof to make certain that the rows are straight. When nearing the ridge, make corrections according to the directions for wood shingle application.

5. The ridge cap is formed by cutting the three-in-one tabs apart to make individual shingles and applying them as shown.

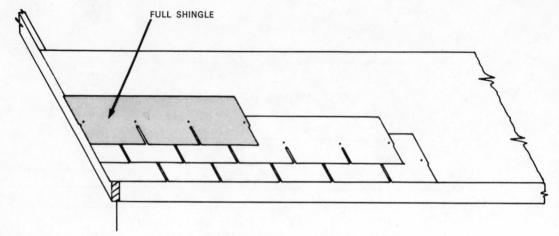

FULL SHINGLE

A full shingle starts the third course.

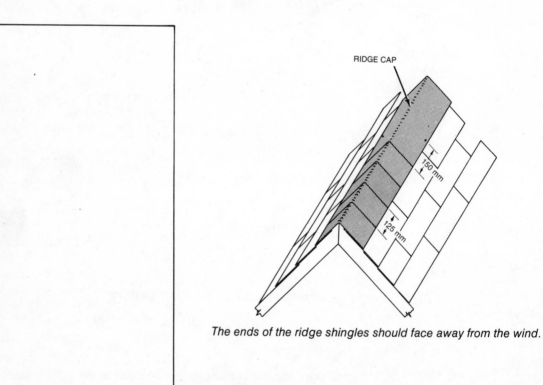

RIDGE CAP

150 mm

125 mm

The ends of the ridge shingles should face away from the wind.

INSTALLING ROLL ROOFING

The slope of a roof often determines the type of roof covering that must be used to make it weathertight. Special low-slope asphalt shingles may be used with slopes as gentle as 1 to 6, but some type of roll roofing must be used with lesser slopes.

Roofs that have slopes of less than 1 to 12 should be covered with two to five layers of asphalt roll roofing felt cemented together with hot asphalt or special cold roofing cement. The last layer of roofing felt is covered with an even coating of asphalt or cement, and fine white gravel is sprinkled over the entire roof. This type of roofing is known as built-up roll roofing. It can give many years of service if applied carefully. The gravel reflects sunlight and reduces the weathering effect of the sun on the asphalt.

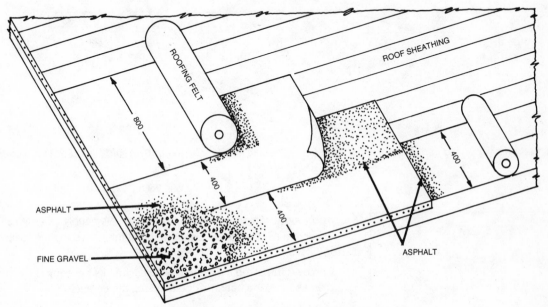

A double thickness built-up roof covering.

On roofs with slopes of 1 to 12 or greater, mineral surfaced roll roofing may be used instead of built-up roll roofing. Like asphalt shingles, this roofing material is available in many colours. The drawing shows how mineral surfaced roll roofing is cemented and nailed in place. The hidden nail method shown gives the best appearance on a house roof.

To install roll roofing:

1. Cut and nail a strip of the roll roofing along the edges of the roof at the gables and eaves. The strip should be at least 230 mm wide.

2. Apply an even coating of roofing cement to this strip along the eaves and partway up the gables.

3. Carefully unroll another strip of the roll roofing and place it along the eaves. Nail it every 50 mm along its top edge and press it firmly into the cement.

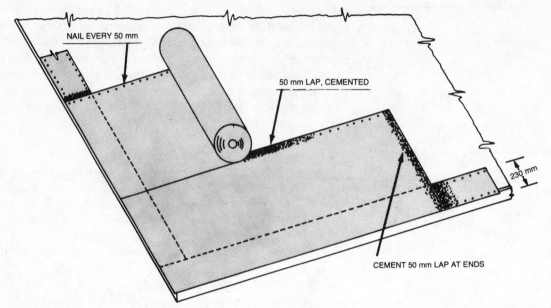

A method of applying asphalt roll roofing that hides the nail heads. The overlap should be increased on very low slopes.

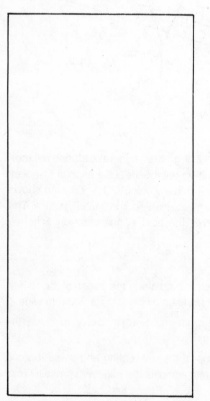

4. Apply more cement farther up the gables. Also apply a 50 mm strip of roofing cement along the top edge of the nailed roofing to cover the nails.

5. The next run of roofing is then rolled out and its top edge is nailed in place so that the bottom edge overlaps the cemented area.

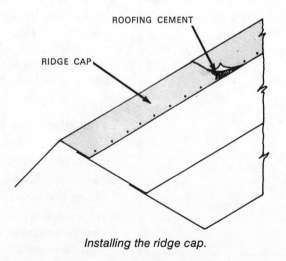

Installing the ridge cap.

6. Continue to apply the cement and roll roofing in this way up to the ridge. Trim off any excess roofing at the ridge. When both sides of the roof are completed, trim off enough 300 mm wide roofing from a roll to make the ridge cap. Cement and nail the ridge cap as shown.

SHINGLING AROUND A CHIMNEY

Metal flashing must always be installed around a chimney that projects through the roof. This flashing must prevent leaks past the brickwork, and therefore must be installed in a particular way. The flashing may be made of sheet copper or galvanized iron.

The roof is usually shingled before the chimney is built. The flashing of the opening must begin during the shingling operation and be completed later by the bricklayer. Sometimes a tinsmith is hired to construct a difficult flashing. A description of a simple installation is given here.

To install flashing around a chimney:

1. First, shingle courses are installed up to the chimney opening and trimmed.

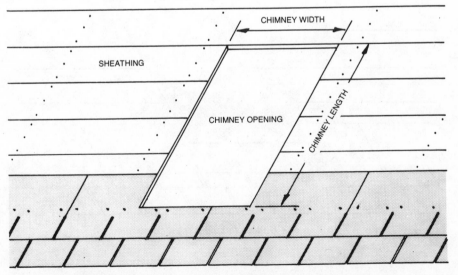

The chimney opening should be measured and cut carefully to size.

2. Cut a piece of the flashing material 200 mm wide and long enough to extend past the sides of the chimney at least 180 mm on each side. Mark and slit the ends of this piece carefully as shown.

3. Bend the flashing along the fold lines and install it as shown. Nail **only** where the drawing indicates a nail head. Use nails made of the same material as the flashing.

   The sheet metal can be folded easily by placing it between two pieces of 38 mm lumber. Putting your own weight on the top piece is enough to clamp the sheet tightly while you push or pull the projecting edge slowly and evenly into position. Do not batter the piece with a hammer. A wooden mallet may be used and will not damage the metal finish.

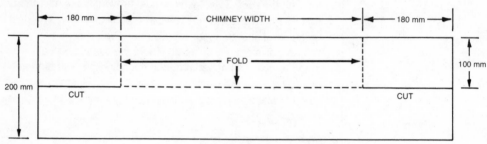

Layout of bottom chimney flashing.

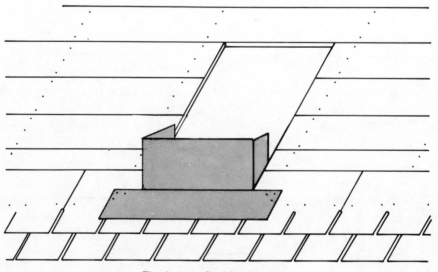

The bottom flashing in place.

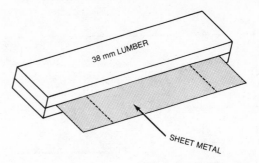

A simple method of holding the metal for bending.

4. Measure, cut and fold two pieces of flashing material 300 mm by 300 mm.

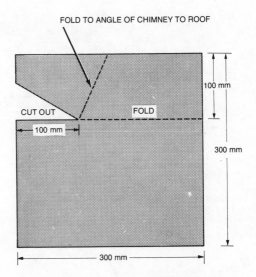

Layout of the lower corner flashings.

5. Nail the next course of shingles in place. Cut and fold two pieces of flashing material, 300 mm by 300 mm, as shown.

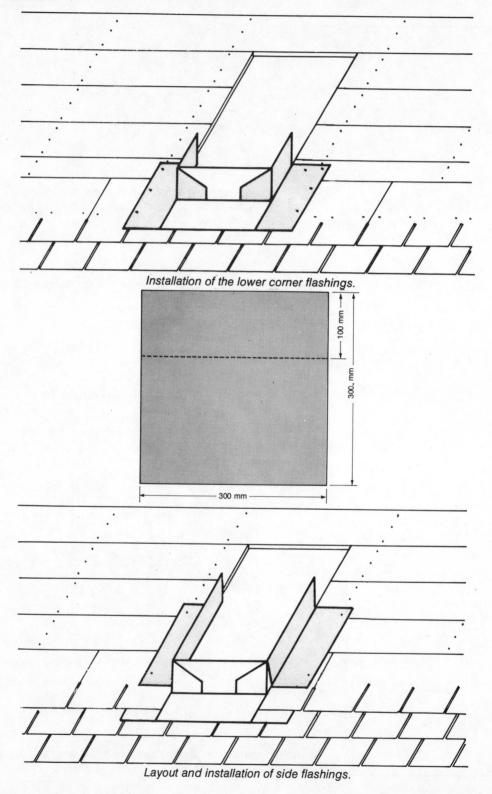

Installation of the lower corner flashings.

100 mm

300 mm

300 mm

Layout and installation of side flashings.

6. All of the shingle courses along the sides of the chimney are flashed in this same way except the last course. For this course, cut and fold the flashing to fit around the upper corners of the opening.

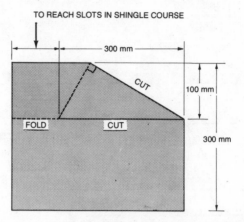

TO REACH SLOTS IN SHINGLE COURSE

300 mm

CUT

100 mm

FOLD   CUT

300 mm

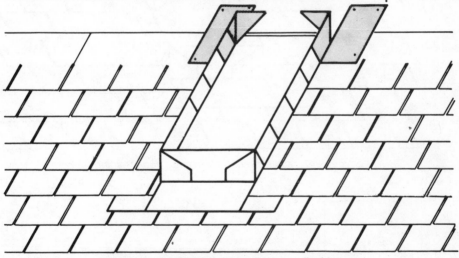

Layout and installation of upper corner flashings.

7. The piece of flashing across the back of the chimney is cut 400 mm wide and long enough to extend at least 200 mm past each side of the chimney. Cut and install the piece as shown in the drawing.

8. All flashing joints should be carefully caulked with caulking cement or **soldered** to prevent any leaks, especially at the corners of the chimney. The photograph shows a caulking gun that uses disposable cartridges of cement.
   A soldering iron and the materials needed for soldering are illustrated here. This type of soldering iron must be heated in a small furnace or with a portable torch.

solder: A metal made of tin and lead. Solder melts at a low temperature.

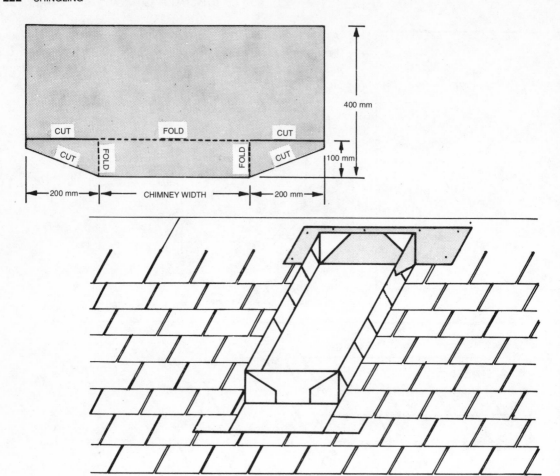

400 mm

100 mm

CUT   FOLD   CUT

CUT   FOLD   FOLD   CUT

200 mm   CHIMNEY WIDTH   200 mm

Layout and installation of the chimney back flashing.

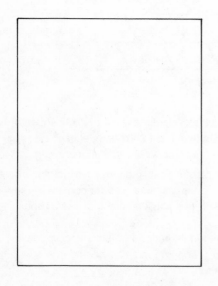

A cartridge style caulking gun.

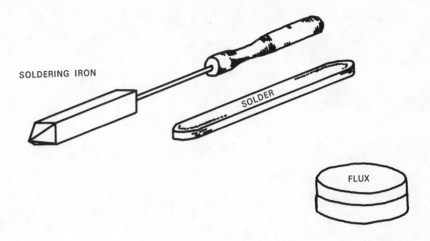

SOLDERING IRON

SOLDER

FLUX

The equipment and materials needed to solder the flashing joints.

flux: Soldering paste or weak muriatic acid used to clean the solder joints on copper and galvanized steel.

9. When the brickworkers build the chimney, they will install counter flashing between the brick courses. This counter flashing hangs down over the flashing installed during shingling.

A completed chimney flashing installation.

CHAPTER 11

Wood Siding Installation

WATCH FOR THESE WORDS

veneer	furring
aluminum	bevel
asbestos	mitre
sash	battens
putty	plywood
asphalt	

HOW TO USE THESE WORDS

1. Bricks are used to form a **veneer** covering over wood framed houses.

2. **Aluminum** is a metal with a low mass.

3. **Asbestos** is used to manufacture fireproof siding.

4. **Putty** may be used to fill defects in wood and to hold glass in its **sash.**

5. Black **asphalt** is used in the manufacture of shingles, roll roofing and building paper.

6. Wood **furring** holds the first strip of siding on the correct angle.

7. **Bevel** siding is usually made of cedar.

8. Siding boards may be **mitre** cut to join at corners.

9. **Battens** are used to hide and decorate the joints between siding boards.

10. Weatherproof **plywood** sheets are used as sheathing or finish siding.

FIND THE ANSWERS TO THESE QUESTIONS

1. Name two kinds of wood used for siding lumber.
2. Name two materials used to imitate wood siding.
3. What is the purpose of putting strips of building paper around window and door frames?
4. Why should the sides of door frames be supported by wedges?
5. What type of wall sheathing is best when wood siding is to be used?
6. Describe three methods of fitting bevel siding at a corner.
7. Name two occasions when furring strips would be installed under vertical siding.
8. List two advantages of plywood and batten siding over board and batten siding.
9. Why should plywood siding not be nailed to the floor header and sill plate?
10. Why is metal flashing needed over some door and window frames?
11. Why should zinc coated or aluminum nails be used to install siding?

Because well-finished wood siding is both economical and attractive, it has remained one of the most popular types of house siding. The type of wood is usually cedar or redwood, but the great number of siding styles and finishes provides the builder with many variations. The owner and builder can choose appealing and imaginative designs. The illustrations show some attractive applications of wood siding. Note the decorative use of wood on the gable of this brick **veneered** house.

Sunburst pattern of plywood on gable of brick veneer house.

Vertical wood siding.

Wood bevel siding.

aluminum: A type of metal having low mass.

Some of the houses built in recent years and many remodelled houses may only appear to have wood siding. Prepainted **aluminum** siding looks like bevel wood siding and does not need refinishing for many years.

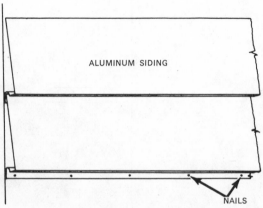

Aluminum bevel siding. Fiberboard installed behind the metal increases the wall insulation.

asbestos: A gray mineral used as a fire proofing material.

When hardboard sheet is cut in strips, installed as shown and painted, it also looks like wood. It is less expensive than ordinary wood siding.

At one time, cedar shingles were popular as siding on smaller houses for a rugged, weathered look. They are now sometimes used to decorate one or two walls of large modern homes. However, wood shingle siding has largely been replaced by **asbestos** cement shingles that are manufactured in a variety of colours.

The rest of this chapter will deal with wood siding application. The knowledge and skills needed to install the other kinds of siding are the same.

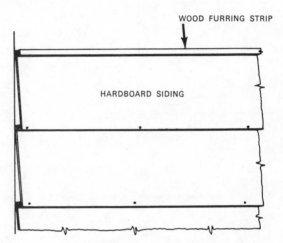

Hardboard installed to look like wood bevel siding.

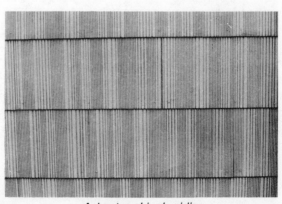

Asbestos shingle siding.

sash: The frame for a pane of glass. The sash is usually movable.

WINDOWS AND DOORS

Before the siding operation can begin, the door and window frames must be installed. Window frames are usually purchased as units complete with **sash** and trim and ready to install. A door frame is usually precut and packaged. It must be put together before being placed in its rough opening. The door frame will be complete with face trim and sill.

To install windows and doors:

1. Begin by cutting strips of asphalt building paper about 250 mm wide. Nail them to the face of the window and door openings so that 100 mm of the paper projects into the opening. This paper will help seal the area around the frame to prevent drafts.

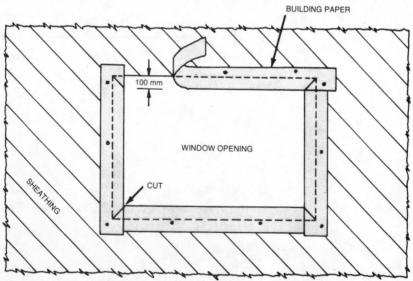

Make cuts in the corners to let the building paper fold into the opening.

putty: A dough made of white chalk and linseed oil. It is used to fill wood defects and hold glass in its sash.

2. As you push each window frame into its opening, level it carefully and nail it through the face of the trim piece to the sheathing and wall framing. Use casing nails and set the heads 3 mm deep for **puttying**. The frame will probably have been squared and corner braced by the manufacturer. The braces must be left in place until after the levelling and nailing operations.

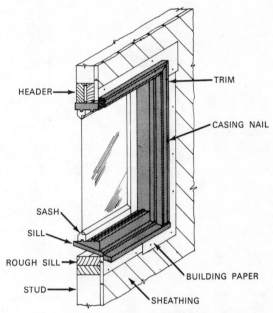

Installing a window frame in its rough wall opening.

3. Since door sills slope down for water run-off, the subfloor may have to be cut away on the correct angle to fit the sill and provide a solid base. Set the door frame in its opening and plumb the sides with a level. Place wedges between the frame and rough opening studs near the top, bottom and middle of the frame to keep the sides rigid and plumb. Wood shingles make good wedges for this job. Nail through the sides of the frame into the wall studs and then nail the face trim.

4. If any window or door frames are not protected from rain by the roof overhang, install metal flashing over them.

SHEET METAL FLASHING

TRIM

WEDGES

LEVEL

DOOR FRAME

SILL

ASPHALT BUILDING PAPER

A door frame must be installed plumb and solid.

asphalt: A tar-like material used in the manufacture of many weatherproof building products.

furring: Narrow wooden strips used to support finished surfaces.

To install bevel wood siding:

1. For increased windproofing and insulation, **asphalt** building paper should be tacked to the sheathing before the siding is applied. Each sheet of paper should overlap the one below it by 50 to 75 mm. Only a few nails need to be used since the siding will hold the paper in place. Wrap the paper around the corners and lap it over the strips around window and door frames.

2. Cut and nail wood **furring** along the bottom edge of the wall to hold the lower edge of the first strip of siding on the correct angle. The thickness of the furring should be the same as the thickness of the top edge of the siding.

3. Fit the first siding board at one corner with its bottom edge hanging 10 mm below the furring and nail it in place. If the sheathing is not made of lumber, the siding nails must be long enough to pass through the sheathing and into the wall studs. Use zinc coated or

bevel: Cut or shaped on a slant.

aluminum nails for all siding application; the heads of ordinary steel nails will rust even when they are covered with paint. The rust will stain the paint. Narrow **bevel** siding may be fitted against trim boards at the corners. This style of siding application is often seen on older styles of houses.

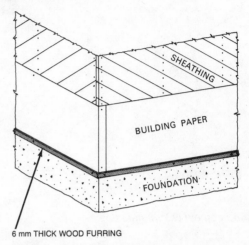

The furring strip holds the bottom piece of siding on the correct angle.

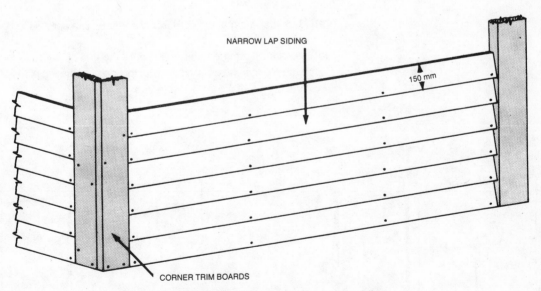

Corner trim boards used with narrow siding.

mitre: Cut on an angle to form a corner with another piece.

Wide bevel siding is either lapped at the corners and covered with sheet metal caps or **mitre** cut and fitted.

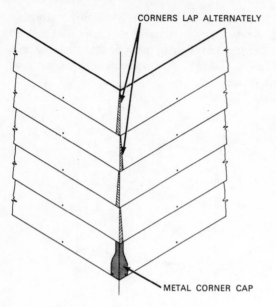

Lapped corners with metal caps.

Each piece mitred and fitted tightly.

A method of marking the ends of bevel siding for the mitre cuts is shown below.

(a) Mark the siding at the corner and square a line across the back of it.

(b) Measure 7 mm from this line toward the end of the board at its bottom edge and draw a line from this point to the top of the first line.

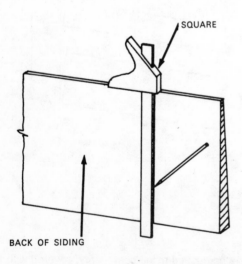

Square a line across the back of the siding.

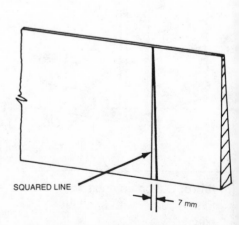

Mark 7 mm from first line.

(c) Mark the top and bottom edges on a 45° angle from the slanted line for the mitre cut.

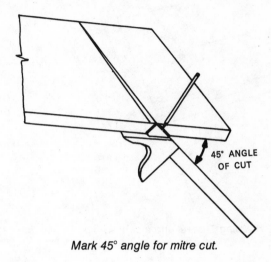

Mark 45° angle for mitre cut.

(d) To mark the cut on all succeeding pieces, set and lock a sliding T-bevel with the slanting line on the first piece. Instead of marking the 45° cut, make a sawing block with two pieces of 38 mm by 89 mm lumber and one piece of 19 mm lumber the same width as the siding. Mark and cut the 19 mm piece in the same way as the first piece of siding. Cut the 38 mm pieces on a 45° angle and nail all three together. A second sawing block will be needed for the opposite end cuts.

Note that the corners will fit more tightly if the sawing block is made with an angle of 44° instead of 45°. Drive two nails through the 19 mm piece so that their points project, and hold the sawing block to prevent it from slipping while in use.

(e) Mark the location of the cut at the top edge of the siding. Mark the angle of cut along the blade of the T-bevel and place the sawing block against the mark. With the side of the saw blade held tightly against the block, carefully make the cut.

4. If the sheathing is wood, the joints in the siding may be made anywhere, as long as one joint is not placed over another. Otherwise the ends should meet over a wall stud so that both pieces may be nailed through the sheathing to the stud. All end joints will have to be cut square for a tight fit.

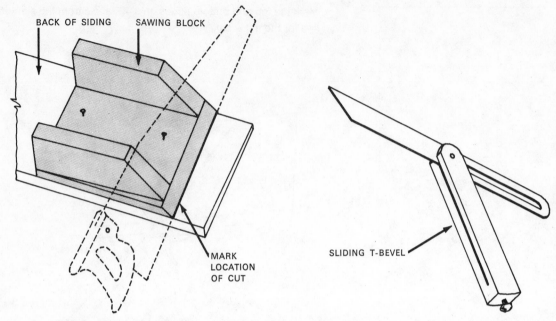

BACK OF SIDING   SAWING BLOCK

MARK
LOCATION
OF CUT

SLIDING T-BEVEL

A sliding T-bevel and a sawing block make the marking and sawing of mitre cuts easier.

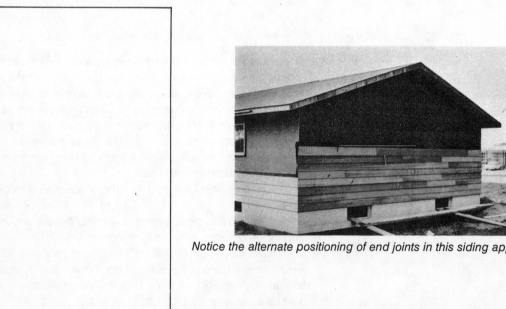

Notice the alternate positioning of end joints in this siding application.

5. Make one or two jig blocks to space the bevel siding so that each piece overlaps the one below it by 38 mm. A nail driven through one jig block and partway into the siding enables one worker to accurately position and hold a long length for nailing. One end of the siding rests on the jig while the other end is positioned and nailed.

SIDING JIG

An easily made jig for gauging the siding overlap.

6. Butt the siding tightly against window and door frames. As soon as possible the siding should be sealed with a coat of paint mixed with boiled linseed oil, or with a prepared sealer. Any open joints in the siding should be filled with putty or caulking compound.

INSTALLING VERTICAL WOOD SIDING

For the quickest and best possible job, vertical siding should be nailed to wood sheathing. If gypsum board or insul-board sheathing has been used, horizontal furring strips must be nailed to the wall studs every 400 mm to provide a nailing surface for the siding.

Cover the wall with asphalt building paper, then nail the furring in place. This method can be used to move the face of the siding outwards to give a decorative effect (for example, a siding panel on a brick veneered wall).

Vertical siding should be tongue-and-groove edge matched unless the joints are covered by **battens**. The surface of the siding is often shaped to make its appearance more attractive. For example, corners can be bevelled to make a V-joint. By alternating the positions of two or three widths of siding on a wall, a decorative pattern can be made.

Square-edged boards with 10 mm by 38 mm battens over the joints are used occasionally. Plywood with battens is now used more often; it has the same appearance and is more weathertight.

battens: Strips of wood used to cover joints between siding boards.

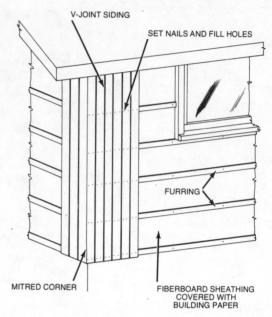

Installing vertical wood siding over fiberboard sheathing.

Furring reduces the setback of the wood siding of this panel.

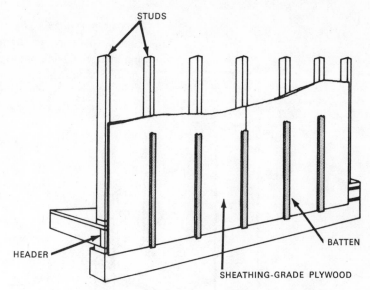

Plywood and batten siding nailed directly to the studs.

plywood: Large panels made of thin wood veneer sheets. The sheets are glued so that the wood grain runs lengthwise and across the width in alternate layers.

In fact, this kind of **plywood** siding in 10 to 15 mm thicknesses may be applied directly to the studs. This makes sheathing unnecessary. If the plywood is tongue-and-groove or lap edge matched, the battens are not needed. Vertical grooves can be cut to give the appearance of matched board siding.

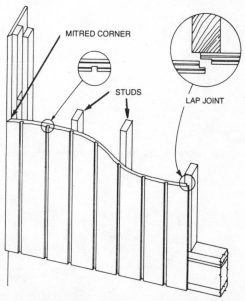

Plywood grooved to look like vertical wood siding. It can also be bought with a V-groove pattern.

Since there is quite a difference in the amounts of shrinkage and expansion between the wall framing and floor framing, you should avoid nailing the lower ends of the plywood to the header and sill. Let the lower ends hang over the floor framing, or cover it separately and install a moulding between the wall covering and the header covering.

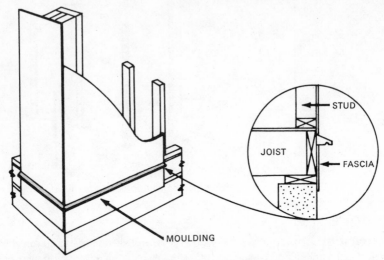

STUD

JOIST

FASCIA

MOULDING

This method of installing plywood siding allows for the difference in shrinkage between wall and floor framing. The joint along the moulding should be caulked.

CHAPTER 12

Bricklaying

WATCH FOR THESE WORDS

mould	porous
cavity	course
kiln	leads
plastic	moulding

HOW TO USE THESE WORDS

1. Some bricks are shaped in **moulds**.
2. Masonry walls are either solid or are built with a **cavity** between the inside and outside courses.
3. High temperatures in the **kiln** are needed to make strong, hard bricks.
4. Well-mixed mortar is **plastic**, and easier to work with a trowel.
5. **Porous** bricks should not be used on the outside of a building.
6. The bricks in each **course** must be in line with the **lead** bricks.
7. A wooden **moulding** covers the space at the top of a brick wall.

FIND THE ANSWERS TO THESE QUESTIONS

1. Name three types of brick manufactured in modern times.
2. What advantages do clay bricks have over the other types?
3. What precaution should be taken when laying coarse patterned bricks?

mould: A box-like container with an open top. The inside surfaces are made to shape and size the brick.

cavity: A hollow, unfilled space.

4. What is a stretcher brick, a soldier brick and a header brick?
5. List three definitions of the word "bond" as applied to brick masonry.
6. What is lean mortar like?
7. What tool is used to establish the height of each brick course?
8. What is the maximum distance allowed between the corrugated sheet metal ties?
9. Why are corner leads built up ahead of the rest of the wall?

The use of brick in building construction dates back five or six thousand years to the settled area at the eastern end of the Mediterranean Sea. Wet clay and straw were mixed and formed into flat slabs which were then dried in the sun. The straw was used to hold the particles of clay together to give the brick strength while it was drying. Later, it was discovered that burning the bricks in a fire made them even stronger and the straw was no longer used. The clay brick in use today is similar to this old fire baked brick, but through the years many improvements have been made in materials and methods of manufacture.

Mechanical methods have replaced the hand methods of mixing the clay and forming the brick. New ingredients have been added to the clay, and other materials are being used instead of clay. Most of the bricks used for the exterior of buildings are still made of clay because of its resistance to rainwater, permanent colours and long lifespan. One new type of brick is sand lime brick. As its name indicates, it is made of a mixture of fine sand and lime mixed with water and formed in moulds. Another type of brick also formed in moulds is concrete brick, made of portland cement, sand and graded fine crushed stone or gravel.

Concrete bricks are produced in a variety of colours and grades that can be used as face brick on the exterior of buildings. Sand lime bricks and uncoloured concrete bricks are also used as face brick, but both of these types are mainly used as backup bricks in solid or cavity masonry walls. The clay brick has more weather resistance and is used as the face brick.

In house construction today, solid masonry walls or cavity walls are not often used. However, some communities have laws forbidding wood frame construction because fire can spread very easily through a closely packed row of frame houses. Solid masonry construction must be used in these areas. Most of the brick houses throughout the country are wood frame houses covered with a single thickness of brick. This covering of brick is fastened to the framing with metal ties and is known as brick veneer. Since this text has dealt entirely with the construction of a wood framed house, only the application of brick veneer will be discussed in detail in this chapter.

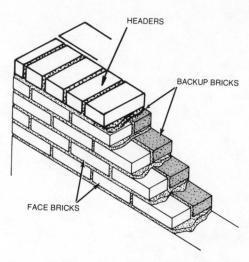

Solid brick wall construction. The bricks are laid in common bond with headers every five, six, or seven courses.

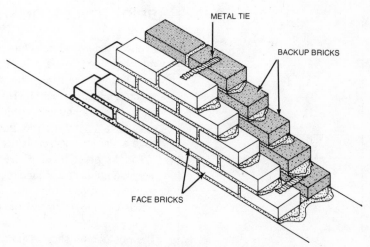

Brick cavity wall construction. Inner and outer walls are bonded together with metal ties.

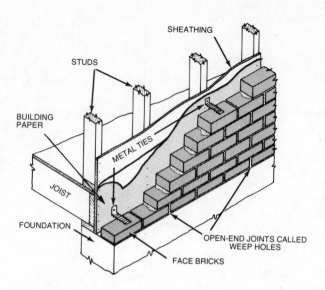

Brick veneer bonded to wood framed walls with metal ties. Weep holes in the first course allow moisture to escape.

BRICK STYLES, FINISHES AND SIZES

In the modern manufacture of clay brick, there are three distinct methods used to shape the brick. The method used affects the style and finish of the brick. The soft mud method uses a soft, wet clay which is mixed thoroughly. The clay is pressed into moulds which have either been wetted with water or dusted with fine sand. This makes it easy to remove the bricks from the moulds. The water struck bricks have a smooth finish while the sand struck bricks feel like sandpaper.

The dry press method uses clay in its natural state of dampness. Very high pressure is used to press the clay into moulds. Because the clay is dry, it does not easily stick to the moulds. Dry pressed bricks are usually smooth faced and frogged.

The photograph shows Roman style bricks that are moulded in pairs and broken apart by the brickmason to show a rough cut edge.

Almost all clay bricks made today are formed by the stiff mud process. The bricks are not formed in moulds. Instead, the damp clay is mixed and then forced in a continuous slab through a rectangular nozzle. Bricks are automatically sliced off the end of the slab with a tightly stretched wire.

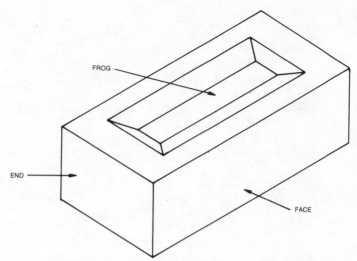

FROG

END

FACE

The face and ends of dry pressed bricks are smooth.

Split face Roman brick moulded in pairs.

The finishes on these wire-cut bricks are applied before they are cut. There are various surface patterns. Some patterns are rolled onto the slab; others are applied with rotating wire brushes or straight, stiff wire brushes that drag on the slab as it moves along. Coarse surface patterns may be cut into the clay slab with rotating knives. The clay is then rolled to fold and flatten the surface. Such bricks are made to shed water and dust. Care should be taken to lay them right side up. Note that finishes are only put on the surfaces that may show: the face edge and both ends.

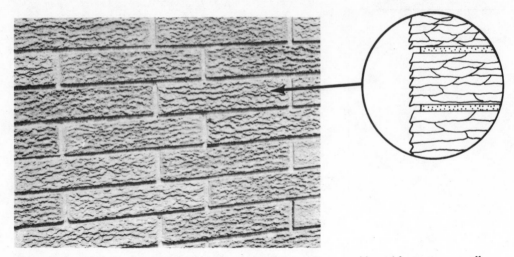

Bark textured bricks must be laid with the slope of the pattern positioned for water run-off.

kiln: A large oven for drying and heat curing clay bricks.

All three types of bricks are stacked and fired in carefully controlled **kilns** at temperatures ranging from 980°C to 1370°C for 60 to 100 h

Examples of clay brick.

Examples of clay brick laid in common bond.

The size of a brick depends on its style. The more commonly used styles of bricks and their dimensions are shown here. About two dozen different brick sizes are available. The standard modular brick is one of the new metric sizes.

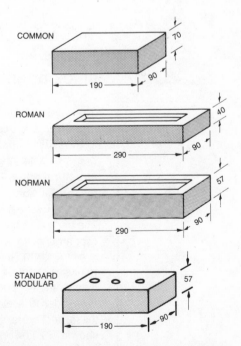

The dimensions of bricks vary according to their styles. One edge and both ends receive special finishes and textures.

BRICK POSITIONS IN A WALL

In solid masonry construction, the bricks are placed in **header position** to tie the wall together. In brick veneer, bricks are usually placed in the **stretcher position**; they can be placed in other ways for decoration. You have probably noticed **soldier course** borders around the lower and upper parts of brick walls, and **rowlok courses** used to form window sills or decorations above window and door frames. The illustration shows these four brick positions.

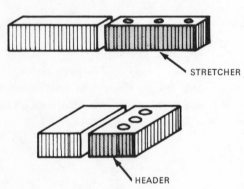

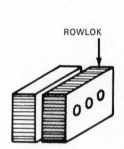

The four positions in which bricks may be laid.

BRICK BONDS

The word **bond** in the brickmason's language can have three different meanings. The design formed by the bricks when they are positioned in a wall is the **pattern bond**. The method of positioning the header bricks in solid masonry construction to tie the wall together is the **structural bond**. The ability of the mortar to hold the bricks together is the **mortar bond**.

In brick veneer work, the usual pattern bond is the **running bond**. The bricks are half lapped and require a minimum of cutting to fit, except around some windows and door frames.

Roman and Norman bricks are often laid in **one-third bond**. This makes a simple corner lap. The width of each brick is one-third its length, and the end joints form vertical line patterns on the wall.

In order to avoid the vertical end joint patterns of one-third bond, these bricks are sometimes laid in a **one-third diagonal bond** as shown. The first brick in every third course is shortened by 100 mm, or one-third of its length. The end joints then form diagonal lines across the wall face.

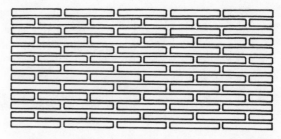

Bricks laid in running bond which is also known as one-half bond.

Roman bricks laid on one-third bond.

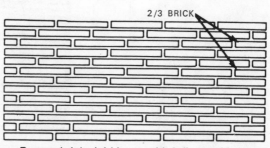

2/3 BRICK

Roman bricks laid in one-third diagonal bond.

When cutting a brick with a brick bolster and hammer, score the brick on all four sides, gradually deepening the scores until putting a little extra strength behind the hammer will cause the brick to break along the score marks. The bevel side of the bolster should be held facing the waste end of the brick. Experienced brickmasons use the chisel end of the bricking hammer to score and break a brick.

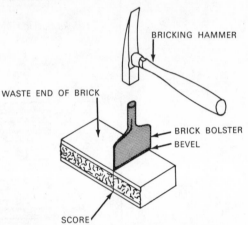

Scoring and cutting a brick with bolster and hammer.

The **stack bond** is decorative and is often used in spite of its lack of structural strength. Corrugated sheet metal ties must be used to tie the stacks of bricks together.

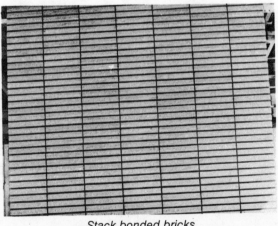

Stack bonded bricks.

MORTAR FOR BRICKLAYING

The three commonly known bricking mortars are straight lime mortar, straight cement mortar and cement lime mortar. All three types include washed and graded sand as the body or aggregate of the mortar. The mortar described in Chapter 4 is a cement lime mortar. The materials must be mixed in exact quantities with carefully measured amounts of water clean enough to drink to make a **plastic** mixture.

A plastic mortar is easily handled with a trowel and bonds well to the bricks. It should be neither soupy nor dry and crumbling. Mortar that will not stick to the trowel has too much sand in proportion to the cement and lime and is a **lean mortar**. If the mortar is too sticky to spread easily, it has too little sand and is too rich in lime. This is called a **fat mortar**. Mix only enough mortar in each batch to last about two hours. If it stiffens slightly before it is used up, a little water may be added and the mortar mixed again.

Straight lime mortar is a mixture of one part hydrated lime to two or three parts sand. This mortar is easy to work with but sets too slowly for the speed of modern construction. Also, it does not have the strength of mortars containing cement. A good mortar to use in class is made with one bag of hydrated lime to ten shovels of sand. This mix does not set; instead it dries out and becomes hard. This lime mortar can be remixed by adding water to the dried mortar.

Straight cement mortar without lime is not easily workable and makes a **porous**, weak joint which does not bond well to bricks. It is made with one part portland cement to two or three parts sand.

Cement lime mortar may be used for all bricklaying jobs. It is made of one part portland cement with one-quarter to one-half part hydrated lime for ideal plasticity and with no more than three parts sand.

The illustration shows the hand method of mixing mortar. The cement, lime and sand are thoroughly mixed while still dry and pulled to one end of a mortar box. Water is added at the other end of the box and the dry material is pulled into it. The more the mortar is mixed with the hoe, the more plastic it will become.

plastic: Easily shaped and handled.

porous: Full of very small holes.

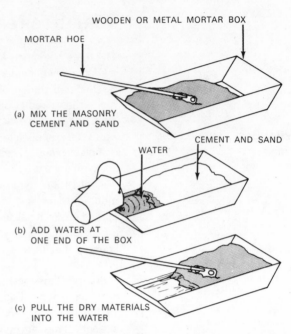

(a) MIX THE MASONRY CEMENT AND SAND

(b) ADD WATER AT ONE END OF THE BOX

(c) PULL THE DRY MATERIALS INTO THE WATER

Hand mixing masonry cement and sand to make mortar.

Once the mortar is mixed, transfer it to the mortar boards with a hod or a pail. Wash the hod or pail after carrying the mortar so that no hard mortar particles will get into the next batch. The mortar boards and brick should be placed near the work being done.

A pail of mortar placed on each mortar board.

BUILDING THE LEADS

course: A series of bricks placed in a row.

First, the sheathing should be covered with asphalt building paper for additional windproofing. (This is also done when wood siding is applied.) The strips of paper should overlap by 60 mm, and should be nailed at each stud with wide-headed nails spaced 150 to 200 mm apart.

To determine the end spacing of the bricks, clean all dirt and wood chips away from the top of the foundation. Position a **course** of bricks along the wall. These should at first be spaced 10 mm apart, but this space may be slightly narrowed or widened to make a whole or half brick fit at the end of the course. If the spacing cannot be adjusted to accomplish this, one brick at both ends of the course will have to be cut. Mark the final spacing on the foundation and remove the bricks.

To establish the vertical spacing of the brick courses, use a brick spacing rule to measure the distances from the foundation to the bottoms of the window sills and to the tops of door and window frames. A brick spacing rule looks like an ordinary metric tape measure, but it is also marked with the numbers 1 to 10. These represent the thickness of the brick plus the mortar joint.

Choose the spacing by the number on the rule so that the courses of the brick being used will reach the window sills, and so that they will rest on an angle-iron support above the door and window frames. The angle-iron supports the bricks laid above the frames. The illustration shows a 57 mm standard brick and a 10 mm mortar joint, with a spacing of 4. In modern, single-storey house construction, the vertical spacing will probably be determined by the window sill heights since the tops of the frames rest against the roof soffit.

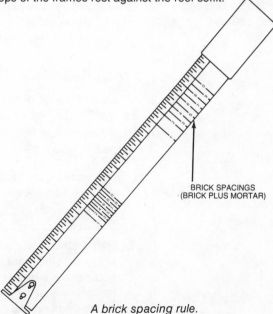

BRICK SPACINGS
(BRICK PLUS MORTAR)

A brick spacing rule.

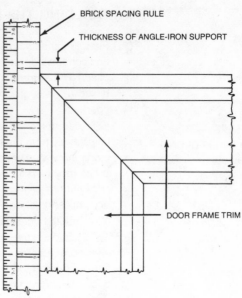

BRICK SPACING RULE

THICKNESS OF ANGLE-IRON SUPPORT

DOOR FRAME TRIM

57 mm bricks with 10 mm mortar joints would exactly fit the height of this door frame.

When the spacing number has been determined, hold the spacing rule against the walls at the corners and mark the spacing of each course on the sheathing from foundation to roof soffit. Construction of the **leads** can begin at this point. Each brick course will be laid to the height of the mark on the sheathing.

If the bricks are porous (likely to absorb the water from the mortar), they should be thoroughly wet before laying. Otherwise the mortar will dry out before it has a chance to harden properly. All sand lime and concrete bricks should be kept wet.

To lay bricks:

1. Using a trowel, pick up and spread enough mortar on the foundation for four to six bricks. Use a smooth throwing motion to deposit a wide layer of mortar. Furrow this mortar bed with the point of the trowel.

   If mortar has run over the edge of the wall, these slops should be removed from the wall with the trowel. Mortar slops on the foundation or brick can usually be removed with a burlap bag or a stiff bristled broom.

2. Position the corner brick by pushing it down into the mortar bed until it is at the correct height and is level. Leave a 35 mm space between the brick and the sheathing. Use the trowel to clean off the mortar that squeezes out of the joint. This amount of mortar is often enough to butter the end of the next brick.

leads: The first bricks in several courses built up at both ends of a wall. They act as guides for bricking straight wall courses.

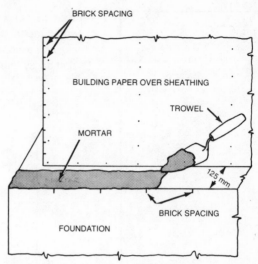

Spread a full bed of mortar for four to six bricks.

3. Butter the end of a brick and place it against the corner brick. Push this brick downwards so that the free end is even with the spacing mark on the foundation and the top is level with the first brick. Gently tap the corners of the brick into position with the handle of the trowel.

   Two separate motions of the trowel are needed to butter the end of a brick correctly. Hold the brick in one hand so that the end to be buttered leans away from you and toward the trowel in your other hand. Tip the blade of the trowel and apply mortar to the end of the brick with a slashing motion. The second stroke of the trowel should press and seal the mortar along the end of the brick at its outer or face edge. It may be necessary to add a small amount of mortar with this motion of the trowel.

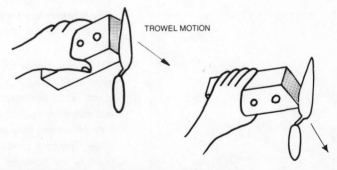

The end of a brick is buttered with mortar using two motions of the trowel.

4. Placing six to eight bricks along each side of the corner, continue to spread mortar and butter bricks. Use a spirit level to check the flatness and alignment of the brick tops and edges. Tap any out of position bricks into place.

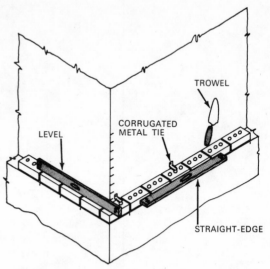

Each course of bricks must be level and in line.

5. Nail corrugated metal ties to the wood framing so that they rest on top of the bricks and are no more than 600 mm apart. Build the leads five courses higher, and again install metal ties.

   As the leads are built up, use the level to make certain both sides of the corner are plumb. Check the accuracy of the end joints with the level held against the slope of the lead. The completed leads will be twelve to sixteen courses high and should be built on all four corners of the foundation to act as guides for filling in the rest of the wall.

6. Before the mortar hardens, the joints should be tooled to the desired shape. The illustration shows joint shapes that are commonly used. Since the main purpose of tooling is to make the joint more watertight, the raked and struck joints are not altogether satisfactory. However, they are sometimes used because of their appearance. The best method for protection from severe weather conditions is the concave rodded or V-tooled joint. These treatments seal the mortar to the edges of the bricks on both sides of the joint.

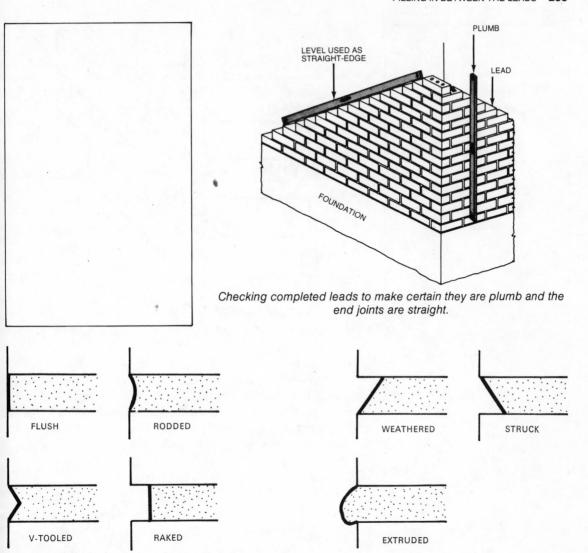

Checking completed leads to make certain they are plumb and the end joints are straight.

FLUSH

RODDED

WEATHERED

STRUCK

V-TOOLED

RAKED

EXTRUDED

Styles of tooled joints used in brick masonry.

FILLING IN BETWEEN THE LEADS

Use a light mason's line as a guide for laying each course of bricks between the leads. Attach the line to a line block and position the block on the corner of the left-hand lead. Pull the line tight, and attach it to a line block hooked over the corner of the right-hand lead. The line should run level with the top edges of the bricks in the lead courses. As each course is completed, the line is moved up one brick space. The bricks laid to the line should be even with it without touching it. The line should not be disturbed while placing each brick.

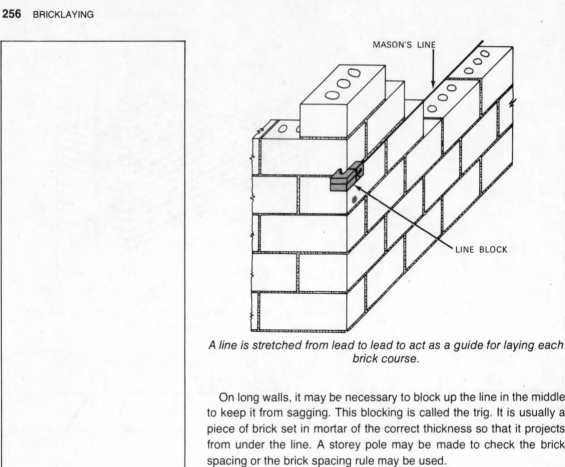

A line is stretched from lead to lead to act as a guide for laying each brick course.

On long walls, it may be necessary to block up the line in the middle to keep it from sagging. This blocking is called the trig. It is usually a piece of brick set in mortar of the correct thickness so that it projects from under the line. A storey pole may be made to check the brick spacing or the brick spacing rule may be used.

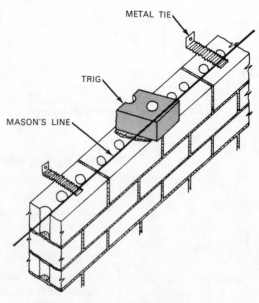

The trig keeps the line from sagging.

The closure brick in each course should be buttered on both ends. The ends of the bricks on each side of the space where it fits should also be buttered. Although some of the mortar is scraped away from these surfaces when the brick is lowered into position, a complete end bond should result.

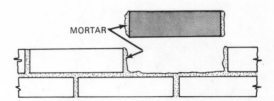

Placing a brick closure. Note the locations for mortar.

Door and window frames are not always exactly the right width nor in the right place to make the fitting of a whole or half brick possible. The construction shown below is ideal. Note that the half bricks are always turned with the cut end toward the sheathing. If a long brick is used, only one-third of the brick is placed in this way.

Laying bricks to a door frame. The cut end of the half brick is turned inwards.

If the space between the last whole brick and the frame is greater or less than the width of a brick, two or more bricks may have to be cut to form a strong and attractive bond.

When the wall area between the leads has been completed, new leads must be built on the corners and the wall built to the top of these. This method is continued to the tops of the walls.

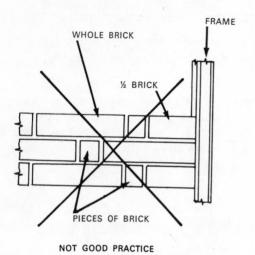

NOT GOOD PRACTICE

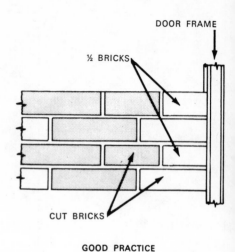

GOOD PRACTICE

The pattern bond at a framed opening should be both strong and attractive.

moulding: A narrow strip of wood shaped to cover and improve the appearance of the joint between two surfaces.

If the brick must be laid over door or window frames, install a length of 6 mm by 100 mm by 100 mm angle-iron across the top of the frame so that its ends rest on at least a half brick. This is not a practical way to support brick above a window or garage door wider than 2.75 m. Wide windows will need a support with a vertical side higher than 100 mm.

The last course of bricks under the roof soffit is the most difficult to lay. A space of about 25 mm is usually left above this course and a special brick **moulding** nailed to the soffit to cover this space.

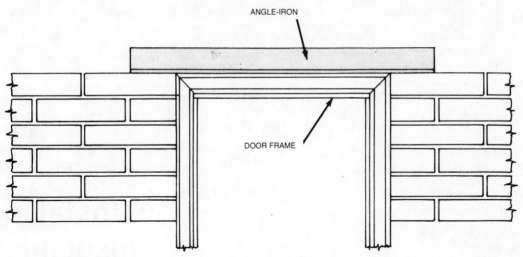

ANGLE-IRON

DOOR FRAME

Installing a length of angle-iron across an opening to support the brick courses above it.

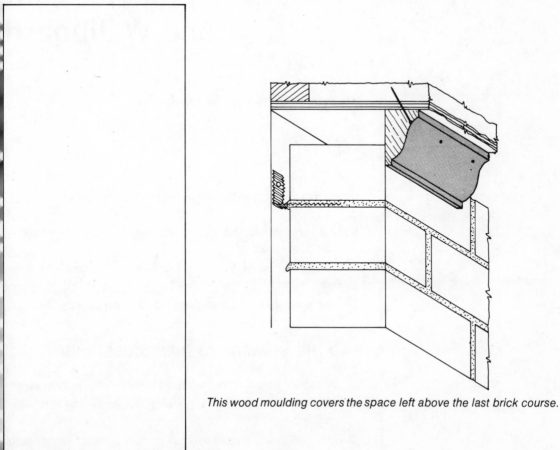

This wood moulding covers the space left above the last brick course.

CHAPTER 13

Installing Insulation, Plaster Lath and Wallboard

WATCH FOR THESE WORDS

vapour   foil
fibre   bead

HOW TO USE THESE WORDS

1. Aluminum **foil** is sometimes used as a **vapour** barrier on the inside of the house walls.
2. Insulation for wood frame houses is made of mineral or glass **fibre**.
3. A metal **bead** keeps plaster corners from being chipped.

FIND THE ANSWERS TO THESE QUESTIONS

1. What thickness of insulation should be installed in exterior walls?
2. Why is a vapour barrier so important to the effectiveness of insulation?
3. Why should lath joints not occur at the corners of window and door openings?

4. What material is used to reinforce the joints between walls and the ceiling?

5. Describe the purpose of plaster grounds around rough door openings.

6. Suggest two reasons why gypsum wallboard is used in many new houses instead of plaster.

7. What is the advantage of using the largest possible sheets of wallboard?

8. How tightly should nails be driven into gypsum wallboard?

9. What is the purpose of the small holes in joint reinforcing tape?

10. How should the edges of outside corners be reinforced?

Work on the interior of a house may begin once the outside walls have been sheathed, the roof is shingled, and the windows and doors are installed.

All of the rough plumbing and the heating system and electrical wiring should be installed in the framing. (The fixtures necessary to complete these systems are installed after the interior wall covering is finished.) The exterior walls and the ceilings in the top storey should then be insulated and provided with a **vapour** barrier.

vapour: Very small water droplets in the air; moisture.

fibre: Fine, often short, thread.

The insulation used in the construction of new houses is a spun mineral or glass **fibre** made up in paper covered batts or rolls. These are available in several thicknesses and widths to fit between standard spaced studs and joists. Insulation for walls should be 100 to 150 mm thick; insulation for the ceiling should be 150 to 250 mm thick.

One side of the covering material is usually vapour-proof, so that moisture coming from the interior of the house is prevented from reaching the insulation. The freezing of moisture in winter weather would cause the insulation to lose effectiveness. Most builders also apply a metal **foil** or plastic sheet moisture barrier over the insulation for increased protection. A stapler is used to fasten the insulation and moisture-proofing materials to the wood framing. Both materials should be fitted tightly around electrical and heat outlets.

foil: A very thin sheet of metal. In buildings, the metal is usually aluminum.

Plaster is an interior wall covering that may be trowelled over masonry surfaces, gypsum board surfaces or steel mesh. The gypsum board and metal mesh materials are called plaster lath.

Gypsum board lath used in house construction is made of a layer of gypsum sandwiched between two layers of heavy paper. It is purchased in bundles of sheets which measure 9.5 mm thick, 400 mm wide, and 1200 mm long. There are six sheets in each bundle. The gypsum core is made of finely ground gypsum rock that has been mixed with water to form a paste and pressed between the paper sheets. It is used as a wall covering because it is very resistant to fire.

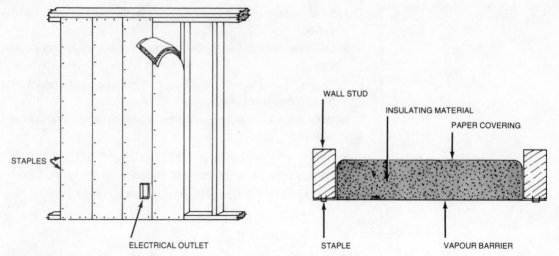

Installing insulation between the wall studs. A moistureproof material next to the inner paper covering acts as a vapour barrier.

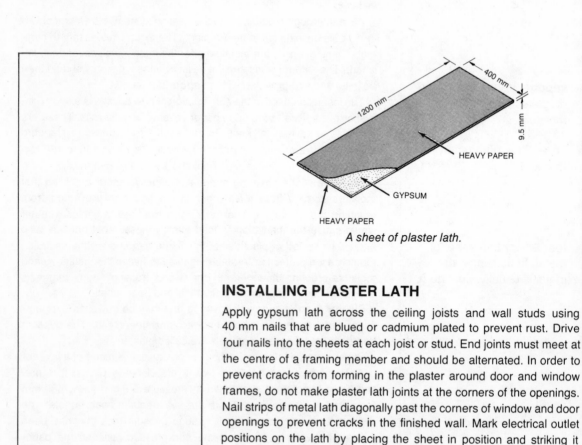

A sheet of plaster lath.

INSTALLING PLASTER LATH

Apply gypsum lath across the ceiling joists and wall studs using 40 mm nails that are blued or cadmium plated to prevent rust. Drive four nails into the sheets at each joist or stud. End joints must meet at the centre of a framing member and should be alternated. In order to prevent cracks from forming in the plaster around door and window frames, do not make plaster lath joints at the corners of the openings. Nail strips of metal lath diagonally past the corners of window and door openings to prevent cracks in the finished wall. Mark electrical outlet positions on the lath by placing the sheet in position and striking it sharply with the heel of your hand. Make the cutouts with a keyhole saw.

NO JOINTS AT CORNERS

4 NAILS
AT EACH STUD

ALTERNATE JOINTS

DOOR
(ROUGH OPENING)

ELECTRICAL BOXES

Plaster lath applied to a partition with studs positioned at 600 mm centres.

The joints in plaster between two adjoining walls, and the joints between walls and the ceiling, have a tendency to crack because wood framing can shrink and expand. To minimize this cracking, you should install a strip of painted metal lath 120 mm wide along the joints. This lath is bent at a 90° angle with 60 mm against each surface. A metal corner **bead** should be installed where two walls meet to form an outside corner. This bead acts as a guide for the plasterer and strengthens the corner to prevent the plaster from chipping.

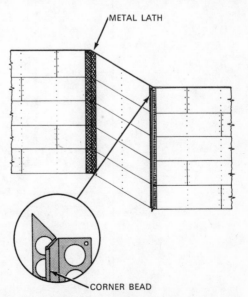

METAL LATH

CORNER BEAD

Corner reinforcement for inside and outside corners. The studs are 600 mm apart in this example.

bead: A narrow strip or band with round edges.

The window and door frames installed in the outer walls of the house should project about 19 mm past the wall frame on the inside. Cut the plaster lath to fit against these frames. The frames should then project 9.5 mm past the lath and serve as guides for the plasterer. He will apply the plaster so that it is even with the edges of the frames.

Rough openings for doors in partition walls are prepared for plastering by installing temporary strips of wood around the sides and tops of the openings. These are called **plaster grounds**. They must be straight when installed; they act as thickness guides for the plasterer. In well-built houses, plaster grounds are also installed at the base of walls. Here they also serve as nailing surfaces for the finish baseboard. They may be nailed directly to the studs and plate before the plaster lath is applied, or they may be planed to a 9.5 mm thickness and placed over the lath. The grounds should be about 25 mm narrower in width than the baseboard. Upon completion of this installation, the walls and ceilings are ready for plastering.

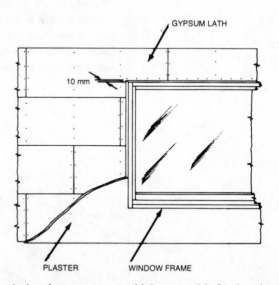

A window frame acts as a thickness guide for the plaster.

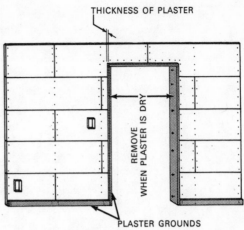

THICKNESS OF PLASTER

REMOVE WHEN PLASTER IS DRY

PLASTER GROUNDS

Plaster grounds installed around a door opening and the base of a wall.

GYPSUM WALLBOARD

Gypsum wallboard is used as finish wall covering in many new houses instead of wet plaster and lath. Imitation wood grained wallboard is often used instead of wood panelling and plywood. One reason for the increasing use of gypsum wallboard is the low cost of both the materials and labour. When it is used in place of lath and plaster, it also prevents much of the cracking caused when wood framing shrinks and expands with temperature changes. Wallboard installation should be carefully planned to result in the fewest possible number of joints. Manufacturers advise using the longest sheets of wallboard available. It should be applied horizontally in one continuous span from corner to corner if possible. Since the sheets are 1200 mm wide, two horizontal sheets will completely cover a standard 2.4 m wall from floor to ceiling. There will then be only one joint to finish on the wall.

Gypsum wallboard is similar to plaster lath. It is made up in larger sheets; one side is covered with ivory coloured paper, and an area 40 mm wide along both edges is tapered to form a channel for the joint filling and reinforcing materials.

Wallboard is manufactured in thicknesses from 9.5 to 25 mm. The 9.5 mm thickness is commonly used in house construction. The standard width is 1200 mm; lengths from 1800 to 3600 mm are available. Two thicknesses of wallboard are sometimes installed crosswise to each other. In this case, the first layer is nailed to the framing and the second layer is glued to the first. A less expensive gray paper is used on both sides of the gypsum in the first layer.

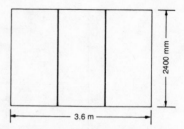

2400 mm

3.6 m

Two joints must be filled on this wall.

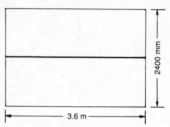

2400 mm

3.6 m

Only one joint must be filled with this installation on the same wall.

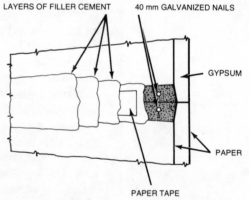

LAYERS OF FILLER CEMENT   40 mm GALVANIZED NAILS

GYPSUM

PAPER

PAPER TAPE

The tapered edges of the gypsum wallboard provide space for the reinforcing tape and filler cement.

To install gypsum wallboard:

1. A bulging or sunken wall is not very attractive. Before you fasten the wallboard to the walls and ceiling, you must therefore check the wood framing to make sure none of the studs or joists are warped. Replacement of these warped pieces is the best solution, but is not always possible. To straighten a hooked piece, saw it through in the centre of the warp, force it straight and nail 19 mm thick tie

strips on both sides. If cross bridging has been used between the ceiling joists, the ends must not project. Also, the water and drain pipes in walls should run well behind the edges of the studs.

2. Install the panels on the ceiling first, using 40 mm nails spaced 150 mm apart. The nails need to be long to prevent them from gradually loosening. This would cause the nail heads to pop through the patching cement. Two people should work at this job so that the panels can be easily held for accurate nailing. Begin nailing in the centre of each panel and work out toward the ends and edges. A wood strip nailed across the wall studs 12 mm below the ceiling joists will support one edge or end of the panel during the nailing. If only one person is working on the job, a T-support placed near the middle of the sheet will support its weight and free the worker to nail the wallboard in place.

   Hold the gypsum board firmly against the joists when driving the nails. Avoid driving nails closer than 10 mm to the edge, and do not drive them so deeply that their heads cut the paper. The last stroke of the hammer should slightly dimple the paper. Since nails can become loose in time, professional drywall installers use Phillips or Robertson woodscrews. Screwdriver bits in electric drills are used to drive the screws.

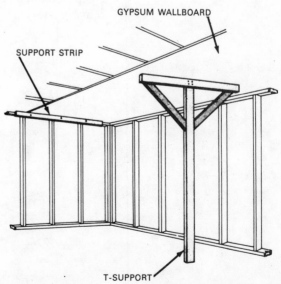

Methods of supporting ceiling panels while nailing is done.

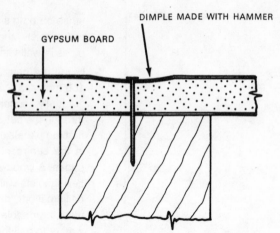

GYPSUM BOARD

DIMPLE MADE WITH HAMMER

The area around the nail heads should be dimpled with the hammer and will later be filled with cement to hide the nail.

3. If the wall panels are to be installed horizontally, you should position and nail the top panel first. Any space left at the bottom of the wall when the lower panels are installed may be filled with scrap pieces, or preferably with a strip of wood which will be covered by the baseboard trim.

    Nails in wall panels may be spaced from 150 to 200 mm apart. To cut a sheet of wallboard, lay it over two sawhorses with the ivory coloured side up. Measure it carefully and mark the cut. Then place a straight-edge along the mark and use a sharp knife to cut the paper. The wallboard will break along the cut when you strike the outer end sharply downwards with your hand. Cut through the back paper to complete the cut.

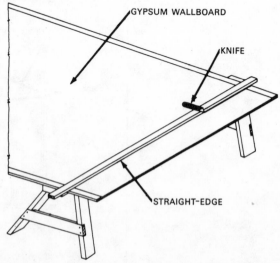

GYPSUM WALLBOARD

KNIFE

STRAIGHT-EDGE

Cuts should be made along a straight-edge with a sharp knife.

Cutouts for windows and door frames should be carefully located and marked. The cutting is done with a hand saw or a keyhole saw. The locating and marking of electrical outlet boxes should be done using the same method as described for installing plaster lath. Rough openings for door frames in partitions may be cut out after the wallboard is nailed in place.

TAPING AND CEMENTING THE JOINTS AND NAIL HEADS

The equipment needed to tape and cement the joints will be a mixing bucket, a 125 mm wide application knife and a plasterer's trowel. Special trowels similar to a plasterer's trowel but slightly bowed upwards in the middle are available for this job.

The reinforcing tape is packaged in rolls that are 55 mm wide. It is made of porous paper. Better qualities of tape have thin tapered edges which are perforated to allow trapped air to escape and cement to pass through. A coarse cloth tape is also available. It is even more porous than the paper tape. A score mark down the middle of the tape allows it to be folded easily to fit into corner joints. Cement filler is manufactured especially for this joint filling operation; directions for mixing it are printed on the package. Use a clean mixing bucket and wash it out completely after each batch is used. Be careful to use the suggested quantity of clean, warm water to mix the cement. Addition of more water than recommended will cause a sloppy mix that may fail to bond properly to the wallboard. Mechanical tape applicators are available, but the following hand operations are usually used.

To apply wallboard:

1. Using the wide application knife, spread cement along the channel formed by the tapered panel edges. The channel should be filled even with the panel faces.

2. Position the tape at one end of the joint and draw the knife along to press the tape firmly into the cement. Cement and tape only one joint at a time.

3. Apply a thin layer of cement over the tape to make sure the channel is filled and smoothed to the surrounding surfaces. Inside corner joints are cemented and taped in the same way, but the tape must be folded at a right angle along its centre score mark. Press the tape carefully into the sides of the corner no more than 300 mm at a time so that it does not buckle.

   Outside corners should be reinforced with metal corner beading made for this purpose. Nail the bead every 75 mm on both sides of the corner and apply cement even with the top of the bead. A second coat of cement should be applied when the first is dry.

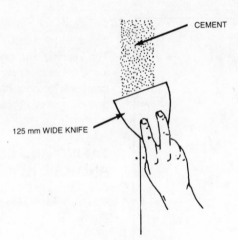

Fill the joint with cement.

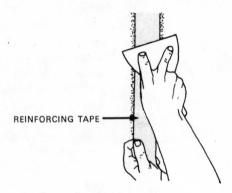

Press the tape into the wet cement.

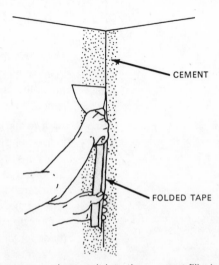

Fold the tape and press it into the cement filled corner.

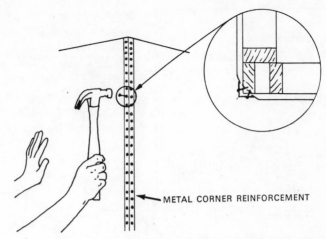

Outside corners should be reinforced with a metal corner bead.

4. Fill all of the nail depressions with cement. The first application should fill the dimples so that they are even with the face of the wallboard. The best possible results will be obtained if one or two extra coats are applied, with a day for drying between each coat.

5. When the taped joints have dried completely, rough areas should be sanded smooth with very fine sandpaper wrapped around a small block of wood.

   Apply a second coat of cement and use a trowel to smooth the material 50 mm beyond the edges of the first coat. Feather the edges to zero thickness with the trowel.

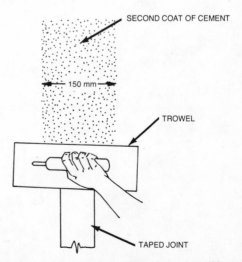

Apply the second and third coats of cement with a trowel.

6. The third and final coat of cement is also applied with the trowel. Make a loose cement mixture and smooth it evenly over a 250 mm wide area, overlapping the second coat 50 mm on each side. The edges must be feathered so thinly that no trace of the joint will be seen after the surface has been painted. With experience, the worker will be able to eliminate the need for smoothing the finished joints with sandpaper; this process tends to roughen the surface of the paper covering rather than to smooth it.